Access My eLab leap4

TO REGISTER

❶ Go to **mybookshelf.pearsonerpi.com**

❷ Follow the instructions. When asked for your access code, please type the code provided underneath the blue sticker.

❸ To access **My eLab** at any time, go to http://mybookshelf.pearsonerpi.com. **Bookmark this page for quicker access.**

Access to My eLab is valid for 12 months from the date of registration.

WARNING! This book CANNOT BE RETURNED if the access code has been uncovered.

Note: Once you have registered, you will need to join your online class. Ask your teacher to provide you with the class ID.

TEACHER Access Code

To obtain an access code for My eLab, please contact your Pearson ELT consultant.

 1 800 263-3678, ext. 2
pearsonerpi.com/help

3624

W138567 (A39015)

LEAP 4
NEW EDITION

LISTENING
AND SPEAKING

DR. KEN BEATTY

Pearson

Product Owner
Stephan Leduc

Managing Editor
Sharnee Chait

Project Editors
Emily Harrison
Mairi MacKinnon

Copy Editor
Mairi MacKinnon

Proofreader
Paula Sarson

Rights and Permissions Coordinator
Aude Maggiori

Text Rights and Permissions
Rachel Irwin

Art Director
Hélène Cousineau

Graphic Design Coordinator
Estelle Cuillerier

Book and Cover Design
Frédérique Bouvier

Book Layout
Marquis Interscript

Cover Photos
Shutterstock © arek_malang
Shutterstock © Rawpixel.com

Dedication

To Dr. Lee Whitehead, my Year 2 English professor,
who suggested I write my essays on what interested me,
ensuring we both learned something.

The publisher wishes to thank the following people for their helpful comments and suggestions:

Karen Densky, Thompson Rivers University

Joan Dundas, Brock University

Bill Hodges, University of Guelph

Heather Melendez, University of British Columbia

Laura Parker, University of Oklahoma

Tanya Tervit, Langara College

Registration of copyright—Bibliothèque et Archives nationales du Québec, 2019
Registration of copyright—Library and Archives Canada, 2019

Printed in Canada   123456789 SO 22 21 20 19 18
ISBN 978-2-7613-8567-1   138567 ABCD   OF10

INTRODUCTION

Welcome to the new edition of *LEAP 4: Listening and Speaking*. Building on the first edition (*LEAP Advanced*), *LEAP 4* teaches language skills necessary for success in college and university. A cross-curricular approach provides opportunities to explore new focuses on critical thinking and accuracy, and introduces new listenings and videos in each chapter. Updated science, technology, engineering, and mathematics (STEM) topics include ethics, innovations, genetics, and journalism. A Critical Connections task at the end of each chapter allows you to expand on what you have learned and apply it to new ideas. Along the way, the Pearson Global Scale of English (GSE) structures *LEAP 4*'s learning goals as you increase your vocabulary with essential words from the Academic Word List.

LEAP 4: Listening and Speaking helps you deal with challenging ideas. Listening genres include interviews, lectures, podcasts, and speeches, and infographics appear in each chapter. Through study and discussion of open-ended questions, students explore different genres and develop the thinking and language skills that are so necessary for college and university. Structured listening and speaking assignments include informal debates, panel discussions, presentations, seminar discussions, and creation of a podcast. My eLab exercises and documents give you opportunities to reinforce and build on what you learn.

LEAP 4: Listening and Speaking will give you the confidence to take the next steps on your path to academic and career success.

ACKNOWLEDGEMENTS

The *LEAP* series is based on an extended conversation with teachers, learners, and education and publishing professionals who share their time and ideas about learner needs to help develop these print and online materials. My particular thanks to all those teachers with whom I spoke at colleges, universities, and conferences this past year in Argentina, Chile, China, Colombia, Czech Republic, Ecuador, England, Peru, Poland, Slovakia, Uruguay, and the US as well as dozens of other countries through webinars. Thanks also to my gracious and supportive editor, Sharnee Chait; her countless suggestions both improved the writing process and made it far more enjoyable. I'm grateful to the entire Pearson Canada team and Pearson teams I work with around the world. And, as always, my thanks to Julia Williams, who pioneered the four-level *LEAP* series and who wrote the companion volume for this book, *LEAP 4: Reading and Writing*.

Dr. Ken Beatty, Bowen Island, Canada

HIGHLIGHTS

Gearing Up uses infographics to spark critical thinking, reflection, and discussion about the chapter topic.

The **overview** outlines the chapter's objectives and features.

Vocabulary Build strengthens comprehension of key vocabulary words and reinforces them through tasks.

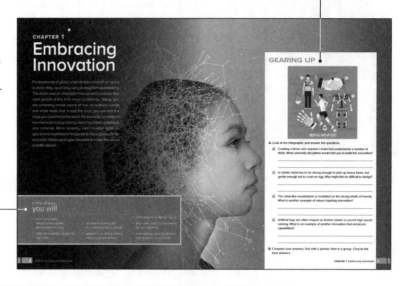

Focus on Critical Thinking helps you learn strategies for thinking critically about what you hear and ways to apply these strategies to listening and speaking tasks.

The **listenings**, including at least one video per chapter, come from various sources: lectures, debates, interviews, and podcasts.

Focus on Listening develops specific strategies you need to fully understand the content and structure of different listening genres.

Before You Listen activities elicit your prior knowledge of a subject and stimulate interest.

After You Listen activities give you an opportunity to show your comprehension and reflect on personal or larger issues related to what you have heard.

While You Listen activities engage you in a variety of active listening strategies, including note-taking.

Focus on Accuracy gives you the opportunity to review grammar points and sharpen your knowledge of correct word and phrase usage.

My eLab provides practice and additional content.

Academic Survival Skill helps you develop essential skills for academic coursework.

Focus on Speaking teaches skills you need to effectively discuss issues using academic English.

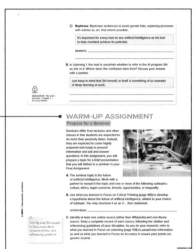

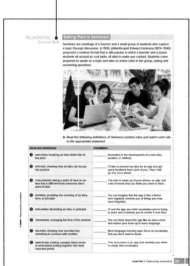

The **Warm-Up Assignment** prepares you for the Final Assignment. Each chapter focuses on a different task.

The **Final Assignment** synthesizes the chapter content and theme into an in-depth speaking task. Each chapter focuses on a different type of assignment.

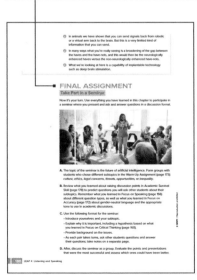

Critical Connections allows you to reinvest what you learned by applying critical thinking to a problem related to the chapter theme.

SCOPE AND SEQUENCE

CHAPTER	LISTENING	CRITICAL THINKING	SPEAKING

CHAPTER 1
EMBRACING INNOVATION
 	
SUBJECT AREAS: business, marketing, technology
	• Listen for repetition to identify key ideas
	  - Recognize signalling words and phrases and learn to omit repetition when taking notes
		• Use lateral thinking for problem-solving
		  - Challenge assumptions and questions
			• Learn ways to challenge ideas
			  - Review and apply guidelines

CHAPTER 2
THE BUSINESS OF HELPING OTHERS
 	
SUBJECT AREAS: business, ethics, technology
	• Listen to recognize persuasive speech
	  - Learn how varied sentence patterns, repetition, and different sentence lengths enhance a message
		• Recognize metaphors and similes
		  - Use metaphors and similes to enhance understanding of new ideas
			• Learn to adapt to changes in conversations
			  - Review change strategies

CHAPTER 3
PRIVATE EYES
 	
SUBJECT AREAS: computer science, genetics, psychology
	• Listen to infer attitudes
	  - Identify words and stress patterns that convey positive, negative, or neutral messages
		• Identify pros and cons
		  - Recognize a speaker's motivation
			• Make counterarguments
			  - Learn about problems in logic

CHAPTER 4
CITIES FOR LIVING
 	
SUBJECT AREAS: environmental studies, technology, urban studies
	• Listen to predict questions and answers
	  - Anticipate questions while listening
		• Predict the future
		  - Explore new ideas to determine logical outcomes
			• Take part in a panel discussion
			  - Learn skills to express interest and elicit information in a group discussion

CHAPTER 5
THE CREATIVE SOLUTION
 	
SUBJECT AREAS: design, education, neuroscience
	• Listen for logical fallacies
	  - Recognize flaws in reasoning in speakers' arguments
		• Explore problems and solutions
		  - Learn to clearly identify the problem
			• Explain abstract ideas through examples
			  - Learn ways to introduce examples

CHAPTER 6
RISE OF THE CITIZEN JOURNALIST
 	
SUBJECT AREAS: communications, journalism, technology
	• Listen for repair, qualification, and elaboration
	  - Learn phrases used for these strategies
		• Evaluate a speaker's motivations
		  - Examine factors that help determine the context of shared information
			• Support arguments with research
			  - Learn phrases for different purposes for sharing research

CHAPTER 7
DIGITAL BRAINS
 	
SUBJECT AREAS: computer science, engineering, linguistics
	• Listen to paraphrase
	  - Learn ways to paraphrase for note-taking and speaking
		• Identify hypotheses
		  - Listen for key words and phrases
			• Improve question strategies
			  - Learn subtle ways to ask questions

CHAPTER 8
SAVING PLANET EARTH
 	
SUBJECT AREAS: biology, ecology, environmental studies
	• Listen to recognize discussion tactics
	  - Learn how to respond to negative tactics
		• Recognize assumptions
		  - Identify and challenge false assumptions
			• Get clarification
			  - Recognize situations that require offering or asking for clarification

FOR COURSEBOOK AND MY ELAB

VOCABULARY	ACCURACY	ACADEMIC SURVIVAL SKILL	ASSIGNMENTS
• Explore meaning and context • Find word forms	• Determine meaning among easily confused words - Learn to choose the correct words	• Learn skills and roles for taking part in seminars - Use the Harkness seminar roles	• Innovate a product or service • Participate in a seminar
• Explore meaning and context • Find collocations and word forms	• Talk about sequencing - Learn words to signal events at different points in a sequence	• Work with statistics - Present numerical data in a clear and relevant way	• Prepare an elevator pitch • Deliver an appeal for support
• Explore meaning and context • Find collocations, root words, synonyms, and word forms • Learn technical terms	• Express beliefs, facts, and opinions - Learn about adverbs, verbs, modals, and phrases	• Measure attitudes with Likert scales - Learn how to collect data about attitudes and opinions	• Explore a topic related to privacy • Discuss privacy in a group
• Explore meaning and context • Find collocations • Learn idioms	• Build cohesion and coherence - Use transition words to show relationships between ideas	• Interpret charts - Learn to point out and explain key features	• Identify two points of views • Participate in a panel discussion
• Explore meaning and context • Find root words, synonyms, and words forms • Learn idioms	• Present reasons, causes, and explanations - Use connectors to build arguments	• Identify problems and evaluate arguments - Learn the steps to understanding problems and evaluating arguments	• Describe a problem • Take part in a creative consultation
• Explore meaning and context • Find collocations, root words, and synonyms	• Learn ways to report speech - Practise techniques and phrases to report speech	• Adapt scientific reports to science podcasts - Compare the structure of a scientific report to a podcast	• Identify a scientific report to adapt as a podcast • Create a podcast based on a scientific report
• Explore meaning and context • Find collocations and word forms • Learn technical terms	• Explore ways to talk about gender in academic discussions - Learn strategies to avoid gender bias	• Raise discussion points in seminars - Learn how to question points in other speakers' arguments	• Prepare for a seminar • Take part in a seminar
• Explore meaning and context • Find collocations and root words	• Use the right tense to express meaning - Review verb tenses	• Examine and solve problems - Learn techniques to encourage participation in discussions	• Analyze a speech • Challenge ideas in a seminar

TABLE OF CONTENTS

CHAPTER 1

Embracing Innovation

For thousands of years, when people moved from place to place, they could only carry or drag their possessions. The wheel was an innovation that solved a problem that most people at the time never considered. Today, you are constantly made aware of new innovations—large and small ideas that shape the tools you use and the ways you experience the world. For example, innovations have led to phones gradually replacing clocks, calendars, and cameras. More recently, heart monitor apps on your phone have been introduced to make you healthier and safer. What could you innovate to make the world a better place?

In this chapter,
you will

- learn vocabulary related to innovation and problem-solving;

- listen for repetition to identify key ideas;

- use lateral thinking for innovative problem-solving;

- determine meaning among easily confused words;

- learn ways to challenge ideas;

- learn skills and roles for taking part in a seminar;

- innovate a product or service and discuss it in a seminar.

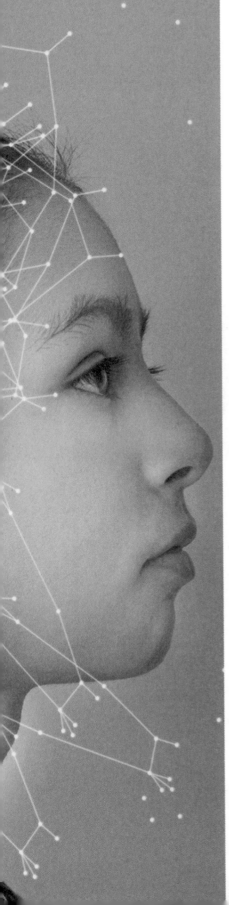

GEARING UP

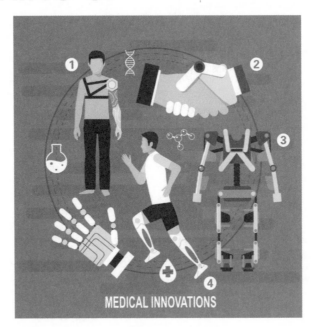

MEDICAL INNOVATIONS

A. Look at the infographic and answer the questions.

1. Creating a bionic arm requires a team that understands a number of fields. What university disciplines would train you to build this innovation?

_____

_____

2. A robotic hand has to be strong enough to pick up heavy items, but gentle enough not to crush an egg. Why might this be difficult to design?

_____

_____

3. The robot-like exoskeleton is modelled on the strong shells of insects. What is another example of nature inspiring innovation?

_____

_____

4. Artificial legs are often shaped as flexible blades to permit high-speed running. What is an example of another innovation that enhances capabilities?

_____

_____

B. Compare your answers, first with a partner, then in a group. Choose the best answers.

Below are the key words you will practise in this chapter. Check the words you understand, then underline the words you use. Highlight the words you need to learn.

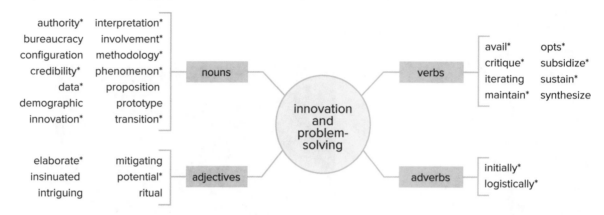

nouns

authority*   interpretation*
bureaucracy   involvement*
configuration   methodology*
credibility*   phenomenon*
data*   proposition
demographic   prototype
innovation*   transition*

adjectives

elaborate*   mitigating
insinuated   potential*
intriguing   ritual

innovation and problem-solving

verbs

avail*   opts*
critique*   subsidize*
iterating   sustain*
maintain*   synthesize

adverbs

initially*
logistically*

*Appears on the Academic Word List

Using Repetition to Identify Key Ideas

You might have read about a presentation in advance or have clues about its content from the context. However, when you are actually listening to a presentation, it can be difficult to remember all the main ideas; you need clues to recognize what is most important. Repeated words and phrases can help you identify main ideas, even if you miss the beginning of the talk. Sometimes repetition is used to stress key words. Other times, signalling words and phrases are repeated to point out main ideas.

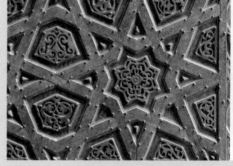

A. Read an excerpt from Listening 1 and consider how repetition identifies the most important ideas. Highlight words and phrases that are repeated or paraphrased as words, synonyms, or pronouns.

*Look for pronouns like **that**, which stand for other words.*

How is "no longer recognizes you" said in other words (paraphrased)?

People are the sum of their memories. And when you take that away from someone, it's incredibly scary. When someone that you've grown up with no longer recognizes you, when someone that you've loved and been in a relationship with for forty-odd years has no idea who you are, this is something that is incredibly painful. There is no cure. But with DementiaHack, what we hope to do is come up with products and solutions that help make life more bearable and less painful.

The first sentence identifies the topic of the paragraph: memories.

Look for synonyms that add variety but express the same ideas.

1 Based on the repetition, which main point or points are you likely to remember from the excerpt? Write a one-sentence summary.

2 What do you think is the speaker's reason for sharing the information in the excerpt?

_____

_____

3 Sometimes repetition takes the form of an example. What example is used in the paragraph?

_____

_____

B. When you listen and take notes, you need to omit repetition. Read the following sentences from Listening 1. Highlight the words and ideas that are repeated, including pronouns and synonyms for key words. Cross out unnecessary words. Then write a short note to summarize each point.

1 ~~So what we've done with~~ DementiaHack ~~is partner up participant~~ teams ~~with~~ mentors who are ~~from the~~ industry, people who have dementia, people who are caregivers, people who are researchers ~~and~~ clinicians ~~and~~ scientists.

DementiaHack teams up mentors, dementia patients, caregivers, researchers,

clinicians, scientists.

2 While a large company can take six, ten, twelve months to push R&D budgets toward something, they're usually stifled by a lot of office policies, a lot of red tape, and a lot of bureaucracy.

_____

_____

3 We committed to do it in quite a short period of time. I know some people who have been thinking about something for twenty years and couldn't even do a simple app. We did it in just thirty hours.

_____

_____

4 For Rodney and I, who have been thinking of this application for managing our family and our role as a caregiver, you know, we just never actually made a priority to sit down and code it out and get it done.

_____

_____

5 I think now, our challenge is to try and find the way of making this a successful, viable business proposition. And as soon as possible, get a version of it that we can get in the grubby hands of our parents so that they don't have to have all the tech calls that we constantly have with them.

_____

_____

FOCUS ON CRITICAL THINKING

Lateral Thinking for Innovative Problem-Solving

Like most people, you probably tend to *dig deeper* when first confronted with a problem rather than try to imagine unusual solutions. For example, paper coffee cups originally had awkward and ineffective paper handles. To solve the problem, designers *dug deeper* by focusing for years on designing better handles. But the lateral thinking innovation of an insulating sleeve solved the problem in a new way. You need to ask, "What exactly is the problem?" The problem with the coffee cup was not the weak handle; it was that the cup was too hot to hold.

A. When you use lateral thinking, you challenge assumptions and questions. With a partner, read the following points from Listening 1 about dementia (memory disorder) and identify a lateral thinking solution for each one.

AREA OF CONCERN	OBVIOUS SOLUTION	LATERAL THINKING SOLUTION
❶ dementia	help victims	*help caregivers*
❷ forgetting to close the fridge	add a written reminder to close the fridge	
❸ dementia victims' anger about being reminded	try to reason/argue with the victims	
❹ encouraging innovation	offer cash prizes	
❺ developing solutions	long-term research and development	*short-term …*

B. In Listening 3, David Kelley talks about his university design course, d-school, and his company, IDEO. Compare the traditional school chair with IDEO's version on the right. How are they different? Discuss your answers with a partner, focusing on how the new chairs allow for changes in teaching and learning needs.

The State of Innovation

A *marathon* is an endurance footrace of about forty-two kilometres. Now there are many endurance events that end with an *–athon* suffix. One example is a *hackathon*, which brings together people with various skills to brainstorm and build solutions to difficult problems. A mix of skills inspires different approaches, and time pressures force people to be innovative.

VOCABULARY BUILD

In the following exercises, explore key words from Listening 1.

A. Find two synonyms for each of the following words. Which synonym best defines the key word?

① mitigating (v.) _____

② avail (n.) _____

③ demographic (n.) _____

④ initially (adv.) _____

⑤ potential (adj.) _____

B. Read sentences adapted from Listening 1 and choose the best meaning for each key word in bold.

① It became a challenge to really **synthesize** the most important aspects because we all had very clear emotional connection to certain parts of the app.

    a) analyze

    b) put together

    c) take apart

② They're usually stifled by a lot of office policies, a lot of red tape, and a lot of **bureaucracy**.

    a) unusual business practices

    b) inefficient private services

    c) complex official procedures

③ Our challenge is to try and find the way of making this a successful, viable business **proposition**.

    a) proposal

    b) investment

    c) reversal

④ You would understand how frustrated we are that we are financially and **logistically** limited to eight.

    a) in terms of organization

    b) computer-like thinking

    c) as intelligently as possible

⑤ And it's also a **data** platform for researchers.

    a) statistically

    b) consequences

    c) information

C. Consider a context in which you might use the following three words. Think of a sentence for each one and share them with a partner. Choose the best examples.

① avail

_____

_____

② mitigating

_____

_____

③ proposition

_____

_____

Before You Listen

A. Listening 1 is about a hackathon aimed at helping people with dementia and their caregivers. The Alzheimer's Society defines dementia as, "… a set of symptoms that may include memory loss and difficulties with thinking, problem-solving, or language." Dementia can also result in antisocial—and sometimes violent—behaviour.

In Listening 1, Shaharris Beh says, "Dementia is not an individual disease. It's something that can tear families apart." What are some possible reasons for this? Discuss your answers with a partner, perhaps imagining what it would be like if a close family member had dementia.

B. In describing the DementiaHack hackathon, Beh explains, "The idea was for teams to get together and come up with tools and technologies that could be of practical benefit to people with dementia and their caregivers."

Imagine that, after an accident, you started losing your memory and couldn't remember where you lived, what your relatives' and friends' names were, or how to cook simple meals. Work in a group and use what you learned about lateral thinking in Focus on Critical Thinking (page 6) to reflect on one of the problems and imagine three innovative solutions.

_____

_____

_____

While You Listen

C. Listen once to get the general idea. Listen again to take notes, using what you learned in Focus on Listening (page 4) to identify repetition. Use the interview notes below to list the key points and make your notes more concise. Listen a third time to check your notes and add more details.

INTERVIEW NOTES	KEY POINTS
1 I'm the CEO and founder of HackerNest. We build …	
2 Like an epic hackathon that was held in Toronto … The idea was …	
3 People are the sum of their memories. And when you take that away from someone, it's incredibly scary. … But with DementiaHack, what we hope to do is …	
4 DementiaHack took place over a few days with …	
5 I'm Lillian. My dementia has caused me to forget a lot of things, including …	
6 Hackathon participants are usually of a younger demographic, usually around like, eighteen to thirty-five. … people participating from all across the spectrum.	*in areas of*
7 Whenever I try to remind Lillian to do something, …	
8 Adore (an app) actually reminds me of some of the things I might forget.	
9 So what we've done with DementiaHack is partner up participant teams with …	
10 This is because we don't want our developer teams building in a silo.	*mitigating this risk by putting teams in touch with the mentors*
11 I think one of the unique things about DementiaHack is the prizing set. … provides winners with support from …	
12 Hackathons are hands down the most efficient and meritocratic way to approaching innovation.	*Hackathons rip all of this away and cut down to the*
13 So let's say I take meds on Friday just by accident.	
14 Without all of the bells and whistles, in the twenty-four to forty-eight hours that you usually have in a hackathon, you are forced …	
15 It's going to be fast, we're talking ninety days where they'll be able to avail themselves to all of this.	*development of the product for market*
16 As Jordan just said, winning teams will have a lot of immediate support to get their idea off the ground.	• *winners connected to companies* • *app that organizes and connects people living with dementia with their caregivers / data platform for researchers*
17 The fact that we had thirty hours to complete the project … synthesize the most important aspects because we all had …	

INTERVIEW NOTES	KEY POINTS
⑱ We committed to do it in quite a short period of time. I know some people ...	
⑲ ... application for managing our family and our role as a caregiver, ...	• *a priority* • *sense of urgency*
⑳ Now we've really proven ... I think now, our challenge is ...	'
㉑ The hackathon compressed every aspect of development to ...	

After You Listen

D. After listening, think of one new idea about dementia to add to what you wrote in task B.

_____

_____

E. Choose the phrase that best completes each sentence.

❶ The purpose of the dementia hackathon was _____.

　　a) to prepare hackers to face disease-related problems

　　b) to develop new solutions in a short period of time

　　c) to cure dementia using a variety of new techniques

❷ The number of groups involved suggests that the hackathon was _____.

　　a) a forum for slow, thoughtful reflection

　　b) a chance for teams to work together

　　c) an intensive and stressful competition

❸ The idea of people losing their memories means they _____.

　　a) should become involved in memory-building games

　　b) need to document their lives with diaries and photos

　　c) can have difficulty functioning and relating to others

❹ The purpose of involving law firms is likely to _____.

　　a) help secure patents for new innovations

　　b) protect participants against lawsuits

　　c) provide alternative employment opportunities

❺ The point about getting a notification about medication is _____.

　　a) to remind dementia patients when to take their pills

　　b) to avoid accidents by caregivers distributing medicine

　　c) to let caregivers know when a mistake has been made

❻ The idea of a data platform for research is probably _____.

　　a) for researchers to review and find new solutions to dementia

　　b) so that these hackathon participants can market their innovations

　　c) a way to keep track of all the hackathon winners and losers

7 The mention of twenty years is to explain _____.

   a) the time for dementia to be professionally treated

   b) the average time a caregiver works with a patient

   c) how a hackathon can get things done more quickly

8 The rollercoaster metaphor is used to point out _____.

   a) how dementia patients feel

   b) the challenges of a hackathon

   c) the responses of caregivers

F. In Listening 1, Beh suggests, "Hackathons are hands down the most efficient and meritocratic way to approaching innovation." The word *meritocratic* means that you are evaluated for your skills, not just your education, years of experience, or position in a company. Should innovations be left to experts? Why or why not? Discuss your opinions in a group.

My Bookshelf > My eLab > Exercises > Chapter 1 > The State of Innovation

FOCUS ON **ACCURACY**

Determining Meaning among Easily Confused Words

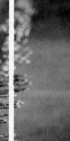

English has many easily confused words. Sometimes the confusion arises with homonyms—words with identical sounds but different meanings like *principal* (head of a school) and *principle* (fundamental truth or proposition). In other cases, two or more words sound similar and are variations on the same idea, for example, the verb *advise* and the noun *advice*. Understanding these differences is important when you listen and take notes. Also, if you use the wrong word, your message can miss the target and confuse your listeners.

A. Read the following sentences from Listening 1 and Listening 2. Choose the correct word to complete each sentence.

1 We have people who are just, who have just been (affected / effected) by dementia in some way, shape, or form participating.

2 And so the question would be, how do you (ensure / insure) something gets to market?

3 (Its / It's) going to be fast, we're talking ninety days where they'll be able to avail themselves of all of this.

4 The more than three-thousand-year-old (site / sight) was a ceremonial religious centre for the Andean world.

5 When you build in a vacuum, you don't actually know (weather / whether) the product you're developing is going to help the person on the other end.

6 If you can control food production, well (then / than), everybody has to obey you.

7 We say, "(Whose / Who's) in charge here? Take me to your leader."

▶

⑧ These underground spaces take you out of your world and put you into theirs, under (there / their) ritual control.

⑨ Their great development comes primarily (right / rite) around the time period of Chavín.

⑩ You know, we often think of archeology as a way to study the (past / passed).

B. Define each of the following words and explain each pair in a sentence. Share your sentences with a partner to check your meaning and grammar.

❶ accept (v.) _____

except (prep.) _____

❷ complement (v.) _____

compliment (v.) _____

❸ farther (adv.) _____

further (adv.) _____

❹ stationary (adj.) _____

stationery (n.) _____

C. Write seven more pairs of commonly confused words. Identify the part of speech of each word and its homonym.

WORD	HOMONYM	WORD	HOMONYM
blue (adj.)	blew (v.)		

MyBookshelf > My eLab > Exercises > Chapter 1 > Accuracy Review

D. With a partner, play a game to practise using the words in your chart. Say a sentence using one of the words and ask your partner to identify which word has a homonym and the meaning of both words. For example, *A leaf **blew** across the sky.*

 **LISTENING ❷**

Manipulation Has Been Driving Innovation for Ages

When you think about innovation, you probably imagine the latest digital gadgets. But innovation is not a new idea. In Listening 2, an archeologist is interviewed about a three-thousand-year-old site in Peru that shows how ancient peoples used stone, water, sound, and light to create a sense of authority among visitors.

In the following exercises, explore key words from Listening 2.

A. Sometimes context can help you understand the meaning of a new word but sometimes it cannot. With a partner, examine the context of the following words in bold. Look up the meanings of ones you do not know. Which are easy to understand by context? Which are not? Why?

① John's research suggests that Chavín society was ruled by an **elaborate** priesthood. Context: _____*not easy*_____

② And at some level, I'm sure that's true, but really the term authority involves the idea of power, but it involves the idea of credible and recognized power. And so, credible and recognized is not an economic **phenomenon**, that's a psychological **phenomenon**, that's a credibility, that's a belief system.

Context: _____

③ John believes that what went on in these strange spaces can provide clues about the origins of **authority** in our society. Context: _____

④ It's an elaborate temple complex that includes an **intriguing** maze of underground galleries. Context: _____

⑤ When we look at the early Andes, these sites that are showing the **transition** to a much higher hierarchical and much more authoritative society, are all temple systems. Context: _____

_____

_____

B. Fill in the table with the missing words and definitions. Share your answers with a partner to check them and choose the best definitions.

NOUN	VERB	ADJECTIVE	DEFINITION OF THE NOUN FORM
❶ ritual			
❷ configuration			
❸			
❹ credibility			
❺	insinuate		

C. Write one sentence with each pair of words. Share your sentences with a partner to ensure that the use of the words is correct.

① credibility / authority

_____

_____

② interpretation / phenomenon

_____

_____

_____

_____

The Giant Marionettes
of Royal de Luxe

Before You Listen

A. Read an excerpt from Listening 2 about the work of archeologist John Rick.

> … it turns out the history of authority and power tells us a lot about innovation and technological change. John's research suggests that Chavín society was ruled by an elaborate priesthood. He's found evidence that suggests visitors to the site were subjected to magical displays of power involving the manipulation of light, water, and sound.

The magical displays were not magic at all, but rather innovative engineering tricks meant to amaze and control people. With a partner, identify a modern spectacle that is designed to amaze the public.

_____

B. A central idea of Listening 2 is how a small group of people can maintain authority through the use of innovations and symbols. How do famous musicians maintain their authority through innovations such as unusual stage routines or costumes?

_____

While You Listen

C. Using what you learned in Focus on Listening (page 4), listen for repetition to identify ideas. As you identify key ideas, make notes on their importance. Listen again to check your notes and add details, ensuring that you understand the correct meaning of words, based on what you learned in Focus on Accuracy (page 11).

INTERVIEW POINTS	IMPORTANCE
❶ We've all had those days at work where we've had a disagreement with our boss …	*prehistoric archeology can help explain why some people are in charge*
❷ Prehistoric archeology is a field in which we're dealing with societies that come primarily before written records. So …	
❸ John Rick has studied the Chavín de Huántar in the Andes of Peru.	
❹ There are labyrinthian (maze-like) stone-lined passages.	measurements:
❺ And John believes that what went on in these strange spaces can provide clues about the origins of authority in our society.	*What's the connection between engineering these sorts of mystical experiences and the establishment of authority?*

INTERVIEW POINTS	IMPORTANCE
6 Well, when you look at the Andes of Peru and you go back 4000, 5000 years ago, there's no strong sign of an organized authority. But by the time we're up to the Chavín period, ... These underground spaces take you out of your world and put you into theirs under their ritual control where experiences could have been assembled, and we certainly believe they were, that would have been otherworldly.	economic resources: psychological control: modern authority: 5000 years ago: transform the very social and political nature of human society:
7 Could you give me an example ...	Lanzón sculpture: strombus (shell) trumpets: water channel:
8 It sounds like it. So, twenty of these strombus-shell trumpets were excavated ...	Sounds like:
9 ... a conch shell and it's exclusively from tropical waters on the Pacific coast running from Ecuador to Costa Rica.	
10 How do you think emerging technology and innovation relates to the development of authority?	To develop an authority-creation machine in the form of a place where you can bring people and convince them, you need:
11 ... development comes primarily right around ...	*the time period of Chavin*
12 ... the problem is that you're not alone. Other people are imitating you and the only way that you, as a competing centre, can keep up with the Joneses so to speak, is by developing your own technologies.	problem:
13 Now what gets very interesting is remember, this is religion.	
14 So does that mean that tools of manipulation are drivers of innovation?	
15 If you look at this, there's a really perfectly obvious example, and that is metallurgy.	the origins of these metal technologies:

INTERVIEW POINTS	IMPORTANCE
⑯ You know, we often think of archeology as a way to study the past of course, but what's the value of archeology when it comes to looking forward?	The real lesson of Chavín for the present day is to:
⑰ Authoritative societies, ones in which we depend on leadership in which we assume authority, we take it for granted and we tend to assume that humans have always been that way, ...	
⑱ And everywhere we go, authority, in the form of symbols, in the form of people, in the form of architecture and architectural settings, is something that we build at some point, but of course most of us are born into these systems. So, I think beginning to look with new eyes at ...	

After You Listen

D. The priests of Chavín de Huántar maintained their authority through a variety of innovations. What they did might be compared to the special effects you would experience on rides at a modern-day carnival or theme park. How do the two differ?

_____

_____

_____

_____

_____

E. Decide if each statement is true or false. For each false statement, write a true one.

STATEMENTS	TRUE	FALSE
❶ Prehistoric archeology can probably help explain modern authority because the principles have changed.		
❷ The fact that prehistoric sites require interpretation means we're only making educated guesses.		
❸ The underground passages at Chavín de Huántar were likely constructed over a long period of time.		
❹ The mention of food production is one factor unrelated to authority.		
❺ The fact that the shell trumpets came from a great distance meant they would have amazed local people.		

STATEMENTS	TRUE	FALSE
6 The phrase, "an authority-creation machine," refers to using trumpets to communicate over great distances.		
7 The phrase, "keeping up with the Joneses," refers to competition.		
8 The development of bronze tools led to the creation of bronze jewellery.		
9 The lesson of Chavín de Huántar is that throughout history, there have always been authorities.		
10 One modern lesson is that we should question the symbols of authority.		

F. Archeologist John Rick mentions that it is necessary to interpret the past. Look at Rick's interpretations and use lateral thinking to imagine an alternative interpretation for each one.

JOHN RICK'S INTERPRETATION	ALTERNATIVE INTERPRETATION
1 The long underground tunnels were used to create mystery.	*The tunnels were used for hiding during times of war or for storing food.*
2 There was no evidence of authority-based cultures in Peru before Chavín de Huántar.	
3 Adornments and decorations were the first reason for working metals, not tools.	
4 People had to compete to make new technologies.	

My Bookshelf > My eLab > Exercises > Chapter 1 > Manipulation Has Been Driving Innovation

G. Based on what you learned about authority in Chavín society, how are the uniforms of modern professionals used to establish authority? Discuss in a group, with each member identifying a different profession and explaining the ways it creates authority.

Challenging Ideas

How often do you listen to a lecture and disagree with what the speaker says? The answer is likely *quite often*. In many situations, you are expected to remain quiet and respectful. In academic lectures and seminars, however, you are often expected to challenge the teacher with questions or points when you disagree or do not understand; this is a natural learning strategy.

> In any challenge you present, remember to remain polite.

A. Below are five guidelines on how to challenge a speaker. Follow the instructions and write answers after each one.

1 **Decide if you want to ask a question or make a point.** A question might be whether there is an alternative explanation. A point might offer an example that contradicts what the speaker is saying. Imagine that the speaker says, "Young people are responsible for most innovations." Write a question and a point you might raise to challenge that idea.

QUESTION: _____

POINT: _____

2 **Understand your reason for asking a question.** There are many reasons for asking questions. You may need a clarification, or you might have missed something that was said. Write two questions, one asking for clarification and one asking for repetition, about Listening 2.

CLARIFICATION: _____

REPEAT: _____

3 **Choose the best time to ask your question.** Ask yourself whether it's necessary to interrupt the speaker before the next point, or whether the question could wait until after the talk. Sometimes a good reason to interrupt is to challenge the basis of the argument. Think of one question you might ask *during* the innovation talk and one question you might ask *after*.

DURING: _____

AFTER: _____

4 **Provide a context for your question.** Ask yourself what makes you want to ask a question. For example, your *background* might include experience with the topic. Your *interest* might be based on the fact that you are going to study the topic. Referring to Listening 2, write one question in which you first introduce your background and one question related to your interests.

BACKGROUND: _____

INTEREST: _____

5 **Decide if the reply answers your question.** Sometimes speakers deliberately avoid answering a question. This may be because speakers do not know the answer or may not want to talk about it for other reasons. In some cases, a speaker might misunderstand your question. Imagine you are the speaker. What might you say to avoid answering a question about Listening 2? What might you say to indicate that you do not understand the question?

AVOID: _____

MISUNDERSTAND: _____

B. Read the following excerpt from Listening 2 with a partner. Pretend you are the speaker and your partner is the listener. The listener asks questions or challenges the speaker based on the five guidelines in task A. After, switch roles.

> **Host:** How do you think emerging technology and innovation relates to the development of authority?
>
> **Rick:** Perfectly hand in glove. The thing is, if you want to develop an authority-creation machine in the form of a place where you can bring people and convince them, you need technologies very badly. You need sound technologies, light technologies, unique construction technologies, and you need material technologies, ceramic production, metals, textiles—all these things that the Andes is wildly famous for.

C. Working in a group, ask each member to think of a popular truth, for example,

- everyone needs a phone;
- video games lead to violence among kids;
- having the latest technology makes you happier.

My Bookshelf > My eLab >
Exercises > Chapter 1 >
Focus on Speaking

Take turns challenging these and other ideas using the points you learned above.

WARM-UP ASSIGNMENT
Innovate a Product or Service

Until the 1950s, shampoo was sold in glass bottles. If you dropped one in the shower, it would shatter and broken glass could cut your feet. This problem was solved by a simple innovation: switching glass to plastic. However, that innovation led to a new problem: too many disposable plastic bottles.

You can innovate any product or service by starting with the question, "How could I make it better?" To answer, you should look at every aspect of the product or service, define the problem(s), and imagine what innovation could solve the problem(s).

A. With a partner, think of a popular product or service that hasn't changed in a long time. Choose something you are familiar with, such as

- a home or school appliance;
- a mode of transportation;
- a common tool;
- a service for choosing, buying, ordering, or using something.

PRODUCT OR SERVICE: _____

*An **invention** is a new product that may be neither practical nor necessary. An **innovation** is more likely to be practical and solve a problem.*

B. Research your product or service and answer the questions. Then use what you learned in Focus on Critical Thinking (page 6) to use lateral thinking to develop innovations that could improve your product or service.

QUESTIONS	ANSWERS	INNOVATIONS
Is it expensive to buy or maintain?		
Is it too slow?		
Is it inefficient?		
Is it of poor quality?		
Is it unattractive?		
Is it boring?		
Does it have unnecessary features?		
Does it have other problems? (List them.)		

Use feedback from your teacher and classmates on this Warm-Up Assignment to improve your speaking skills.

C. Consider how you can share this information in the Final Assignment seminar. On a separate page, prepare notes on the key problems and innovations you believe would solve them.

D. Take turns explaining your points to your partner and look for areas where you can improve. Keep your notes for the Final Assignment.

LISTENING ❸
VIDEO

Design Thinking

While many good ideas seem obvious, they are often the result of a long process. This is true at David Kelley's company, IDEO, and the university design-thinking program he founded, d.school. Kelley's approach relies heavily on lateral thinking, or looking for new solutions instead of small changes to old products and services.

VOCABULARY BUILD

In the following exercises, explore key words from Listening 3.

A. Many words have noun, verb, and adverb forms that tend to have a common meaning. Complete the chart, looking up the words and definitions you do not know, then compare your answers with a partner.

NOUN	VERB	ADVERB	GENERAL DEFINITION
1 innovation			*improvement*
2 involvement			
3	iterating		
4 methodology			
5 prototype			

B. With a partner, think of one other word related to each of the following words. Take turns using each of the key words and related words in sentences, and then have your partner give a general definition of the key word.

1 critique (n.) _____

GENERAL DEFINITION: _____

2 maintain (v.) _____

GENERAL DEFINITION: _____

3 opts (v.) _____

GENERAL DEFINITION: _____

4 subsidize (v.) _____

GENERAL DEFINITION: _____

5 sustain (v.) _____

GENERAL DEFINITION: _____

My Bookshelf > My eLab >
Exercises > Chapter 1 >
Vocabulary Review

Before You Listen

A. Read the excerpt from Listening 3 of David Kelley speaking about empathizing—imagining yourself in the place of other people to assess how they feel. After, answer the questions.

> You know, so I gave my present students their project and it's improved the experience of taking the train from Palo Alto to San Francisco. So the empathize phase would be, ride the train, talk to the conductor, watch people buy tickets, go into people's homes and see how they decide which train to take, you know, look at the signs on how you get out of the train in San Francisco, but just be in the middle of it and be, you know, open-minded to watching people and see what they do, where they have troubles, and what they care about.

1 How could you summarize the importance Kelley places on empathy in design thinking?

_____

_____

_____

2 In Focus on Listening (page 4), you learned about the use of repetition to identify key ideas. Is that what Kelley is doing here? Explain.

_____

_____

_____

3 What is an example of a service you use that you think could be improved? How?

_____

_____

_____

B. A diagram used by IDEO illustrates a design process based on desirability, feasibility, and viability. In a group, ask each member to think of a new innovation that they desire. Decide whether the new innovation could be feasible and viable.

MY DESIRED INNOVATION:

_____

_____

☐ FEASIBLE   ☐ VIABLE

Begin

DESIRABILITY
What do people desire?

FEASIBILITY
What is technically and organizationally feasible?

VIABILITY
What can be financially viable?

Adapted from *The Field Guide to Human-Centered Design,* IDEO.org, 2015.

While You Listen

C. Listen to David Kelley explain his design process in five steps. For each step, write a definition of what Kelley means and outline the example that he uses to explain it. Listen again and list one or more questions you have about each step.

STEP 1 EMPATHIZE

• DEFINITION: _____

_____

• EXAMPLES: _____

_____

• QUESTIONS: _____

_____

STEP 2 DEFINE

• DEFINITION: _____

_____

• EXAMPLES: _____

_____

• QUESTIONS: _____

_____

STEP 3 IDEATE

• DEFINITION: _____

_____

• EXAMPLE: none

_____

• QUESTIONS: _____

_____

STEP 4 PROTOTYPE

• DEFINITION: _____

_____

• EXAMPLE: _____

_____

• QUESTIONS: _____

_____

STEP 5 TEST

• DEFINITION: _____

_____

• EXAMPLE: _____

_____

• QUESTIONS: _____

_____

After You Listen

D. In Focus on Speaking (page 18), you learned about challenging ideas. Working with a partner, consider David Kelley's five steps and how you would apply them to the problem of bicycle theft.

PROBLEM: BICYCLE THEFT	
STEPS	
1 EMPATHIZE	
2 DEFINE	
3 IDEATE	
4 PROTOTYPE	
5 TEST	

E. The following is a list of some of IDEO's recent projects. What problem does each solve? Does each one show lateral thinking? Why or why not? Discuss with a partner.

1 A walking/cycling tricycle for seniors and their groceries

_____

_____

2 A set of snap-together plastic blocks for teaching young children coding

_____

_____

3 A modular vertical indoor farm that looks like a set of shelves

_____

_____

4 Instagran, a service that feeds personal Instagram images on television sets for people's grandparents

_____

_____

My Bookshelf > My eLab >
Exercises > Chapter 1 >
Design Thinking

F. There is no need to become a professional designer to apply Kelley's principles to think of innovative solutions. Would you be likely to apply the principles you learned in Listening 3 to problems you encounter in your life? Why or why not? Discuss your reasons with a partner, using examples.

Academic
Survival Skill

Taking Part in Seminars

Seminars are meetings of a teacher and a small group of students who explore a topic through discussion. In 1930, philanthropist Edward Harkness (1874–1940) proposed a seminar format that is still popular, in which a teacher and a dozen students sit around an oval table, all able to make eye contact. Students come prepared to speak on a topic and take on active roles in the group, asking and answering questions.

A. Read the following definitions of Harkness seminar roles and match each role to the appropriate statement.

ROLES AND DEFINITIONS	STATEMENTS
❶ ANALYZING: breaking an idea down into its key parts	_____ Innovation is the development of a new idea, product, or method.
❷ APPLYING: showing how an idea can be put into practice	_____ I'd like to present my idea for an app and get quick feedback from each of you. Then I will go into more detail.
❸ CHALLENGING: taking a point of view on an idea that is different from someone else's point of view	_____ The idea is made up of your phone, an app, and a list of words that you think you need to learn.
❹ DEFINING: providing the meaning of an idea, term, or principle	_____ You can imagine that the app is like a friend who regularly reminds you of things you may have forgotten.
❺ EXPLAINING: illustrating an idea or principle	_____ To use the app, you enter vocabulary you're trying to learn and it reminds you to review it over time.
❻ ORGANIZING: arranging the flow of the seminar	_____ You can think about this app like an alarm clock that wakes your brain up to learn language.
❼ RELATING: showing how one idea has something in common with another	_____ Most language learning apps focus on vocabulary that you don't need to know.
❽ SIMPLIFYING: making complex ideas easier to understand; putting together the most important points	_____ This innovation is an app that reminds you when to study new vocabulary.

B. In Listening 3, David Kelley talks about getting students to consider problems and solutions related to taking the train. Use your own experience with public transportation to list points you might discuss according to each of the Harkness seminar roles.

ROLES	POINTS
1 ANALYZING	• *public transportation is often overcrowded*
2 APPLYING	• *smaller, faster trains*
3 CHALLENGING	• *the ideas might be too expensive* • *too* • *too*
4 DEFINING	• *The term public transportation includes trains,*
5 EXPLAINING	• *A city needs public transportation*
6 ORGANIZING	• *Let's hear one idea from each person before discussing the points.*
7 RELATING	• *Ferries and trains are similar because*
8 SIMPLIFYING	• *If we look at the ticketing part of the public transportation problem, we can see*

FINAL ASSIGNMENT

Participate in a Seminar

Now it's your turn. Use everything you have learned in this chapter to participate in a seminar.

A. The topic of the seminar is innovations. Form groups to discuss the problems and innovations of the product or service you identified in the Warm-Up Assignment.

B. Take turns introducing your topics. Use what you learned in Focus on Accuracy (page 11) to ensure you are using the correct words to describe your product and service. As others introduce their points, use what you learned in Focus on Listening (page 4) to identify repetition. Take notes on the most important ideas.

C. Once everyone has had a chance to speak, use the Harkness seminar roles and skills you learned in Academic Survival Skill (page 25) to share ideas and ask questions. In particular, use what you learned in Focus on Speaking (page 18) to challenge ideas you disagree with.

D. After everyone has presented their product and service innovations, try to identify the three that are most likely to succeed. Offer any additional ideas that might improve the three innovations.

E. After, discuss the seminar as a group and evaluate which points and parts of the presentations were the most successful and how others could have been improved.

Critical Connections

Would you buy an umbrella that had a built-in flashlight? You might; they're not uncommon. How about an umbrella that also had a pepper spray feature to deter attackers? What if this umbrella could also be used as a flotation device if you fell off a boat, and had a built-in whistle to call for help? Would you be interested?

There's no end to the innovations you can think of, but each one adds to the cost (viability) and some might be impossible to implement (feasibility). Also, many innovations can be irritating and useless.

A. With a partner, look at the items in the illustration and choose one. Use what you learned in Focus on Critical Thinking (page 6) to brainstorm three lateral thinking innovations you could add to the item you chose. Make notes on why each would be a good idea.

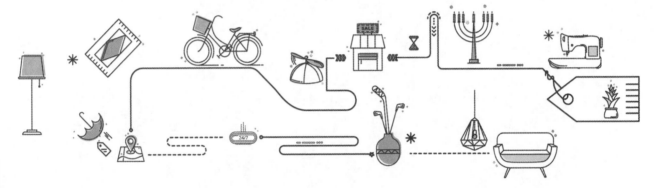

B. Share your ideas in a group. Use what you learned in Focus on Speaking (page 18) to challenge others' ideas.

C. In your group, reflect on each of the ideas for innovations. Are there some general reasons why some might fail? Are there reasons why others might succeed?

D. In your group, choose the best one or two ideas. Would you want to create a business to make and sell the new product? Why or why not?

CHAPTER 2

The Business of Helping Others

Can you think of any large or small things you could do to make the world a better place? Countless individuals and organizations recognize social issues and other injustices in the world and find ways to do something about them. Increasingly, people with an understanding of business are in a position to help make change happen by applying their professional expertise: they become informed, clearly identify problems, plan ways to address those problems, and find people and resources to achieve their goals. How could you become an agent of change in the world?

In this chapter,
you will

- learn vocabulary related to business and social issues;

- listen to recognize persuasive speech;

- use metaphors and similes in critical thinking;

- talk about sequencing;

- learn to adapt to changes in conversations;

- use statistics to make numbers memorable;

- prepare an elevator pitch and deliver a proposal to appeal for support.

GEARING UP

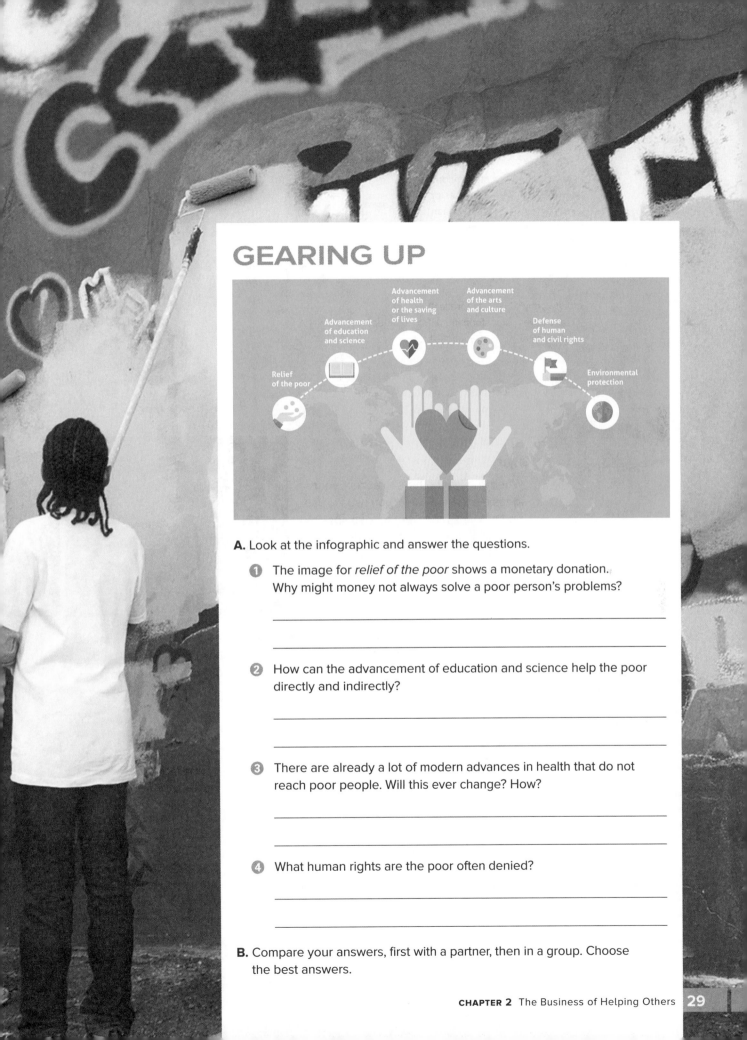

A. Look at the infographic and answer the questions.

1. The image for *relief of the poor* shows a monetary donation. Why might money not always solve a poor person's problems?

   _____

   _____

2. How can the advancement of education and science help the poor directly and indirectly?

   _____

   _____

3. There are already a lot of modern advances in health that do not reach poor people. Will this ever change? How?

   _____

   _____

4. What human rights are the poor often denied?

   _____

   _____

B. Compare your answers, first with a partner, then in a group. Choose the best answers.

Below are the key words you will practise in this chapter. Check the words you understand, then underline the words you use. Highlight the words you need to learn.

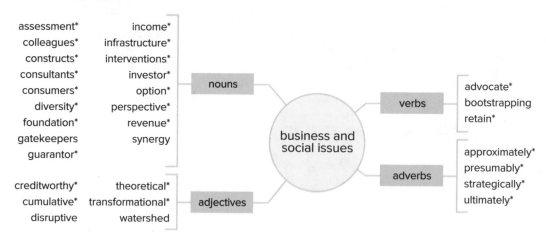

nouns

assessment*
colleagues*
constructs*
consultants*
consumers*
diversity*
foundation*
gatekeepers
guarantor*

income*
infrastructure*
interventions*
investor*
option*
perspective*
revenue*
synergy

business and
social issues

verbs

advocate*
bootstrapping
retain*

adverbs

approximately*
presumably*
strategically*
ultimately*

adjectives

creditworthy*
cumulative*
disruptive

theoretical*
transformational*
watershed

*Appears on the Academic Word List

FOCUS ON LISTENING

Recognizing Persuasive Speech

When you want others to accept your ideas or points of view, you usually use persuasive speech. Persuasive speech often includes emotional words and varied sentence patterns that use rhythm to change people's minds.

Apartheid refers to the racist laws that discriminated against South Africa's majority black population between 1948 and 1991.

A. In 2005, Nelson Mandela (1918–2013) gave a short speech in which he talked about eliminating poverty in the developing world. Read the excerpt aloud. Underline the words and phrases that add force to Mandela's message.

Image of poverty created by placing it in direct comparison to prison

Definition of overcoming poverty strengthened by contrasting what it "is not" with what it "is"

Circular structure to emphasize the main idea, with the conclusion referring back to the opening image of poverty as imprisonment

"But in this new century, millions of people in the world's poorest countries remain imprisoned, enslaved, and in chains. They are trapped in the prison of poverty. It is time to set them free.
Like slavery and apartheid, poverty is not natural. It is man-made and it can be overcome and eradicated by the actions of human beings.
And overcoming poverty is not a gesture of charity. It is an act of justice. It is the protection of a fundamental human right, the right to dignity and a decent life. While poverty persists, there is no true freedom."

Sequence of expressions with similar meanings to add force

Necessary action suggested by a short, direct sentence

Longer sentences contrast with short, sharp sentences before and after, to keep audience's attention

Repetition of "right" to add force

Mandela, N. (2005, February 3). *In full: Mandela's poverty speech.* Retrieved from http://news.bbc.co.uk/2/hi/uk_news/politics/4232603.stm

B. Consider how the patterns of words, use of repetition, and different sentence lengths help to add force to Mandela's message. Does he make a convincing connection between poverty on the one hand, and slavery and apartheid on the other? Why or why not? Discuss with a partner.

C. Read an excerpt from Listening 3 about terrorism and answer the questions.

> I believe terrorism cannot be won by military action. Terrorism must be condemned in the strongest possible language. We must stand solidly against it and find all the means to end it. We must address the root cause of terrorism to end terrorism for all time to come. I believe that putting resources into improving the lives of the poor is a better strategy than spending it on guns.

1 What problem is the speaker addressing?

_____

2 What solution does the speaker propose?

_____

3 What persuasive techniques does the speaker use to make his points more effective?

_____

FOCUS ON CRITICAL THINKING

Thinking in Metaphors and Similes

Metaphors and similes are powerful tools that can help people understand new ideas by relating them to something they already know. Metaphors say one thing *is* another thing; similes connect ideas with words such as *like*. Metaphors tend to use images that you can visualize while similes usually compare two things that have one element in common but that are otherwise different.

In Listening 2, a speaker describes a robot interface with these words: "So their face appears on the tablet screen just *like* a video Skype call." In this example, comparing the computer's face and Skype is only useful if you are familiar with Skype. A metaphor might be, "The robot's interface is a window to other people."

A. Sometimes extended metaphors and similes are combined and build an idea over several sentences. Read the following excerpt from Listening 3 and answer the questions.

The word like *shows a simile.*

Saying what will happen on the highway extends the comparison.

> To me, globalization is <u>like</u> a hundred-lane highway, criss-crossing the world. If <u>it is</u> a free-for-all highway, <u>its lanes will be taken over by the giant trucks from powerful economies</u>. Bangladeshi rickshaw will be thrown off the highway. <u>In order to have a win-win globalization we must have traffic rules, traffic police, and traffic authority for this global highway.</u>

The phrase it is *indicates a metaphor.*

The final sentence extends the comparison with further details.

1 What two things are being compared?

_____

2 How is the comparison extended to vehicles?

_____

3 How else is the comparison extended?

_____

B. With a partner, think of metaphors or similes to compare some of the issues that will be discussed in Listening 1 and Listening 2.

1 struggles of getting food from farms to markets

_____

2 challenges in creating new start-ups

_____

3 court battles to get legal documents approved

_____

When you hear someone use a metaphor or simile in an argument, carefully consider how the comparison might *not* apply. For example, if someone shares the simile, "Education is like planting a seed in a garden," you could argue that many students learn on their own and, when you plant a seed, you have a clear expectation of what will result, while education often leads us in different directions and to different ideas.

C. Imagine someone shared this metaphor: "Poverty is a bottomless hole." In what ways is this a good or bad comparison? How do metaphors or similes improve presentations or discussions? Exchange your ideas in a group and try to find a better metaphor or simile for poverty.

 **LISTENING ❶** **VIDEO**

Reimagining Business in Latin America

Living in the modern world, it's easy to imagine that technology is improving everyone's life. But many jobs still require long hours and hard work. Some social entrepreneurs are looking at age-old problems and finding solutions.

Cali, Colombia

VOCABULARY BUILD

In the following exercises, explore key words from Listening 1.

A. Consider the context and meaning of the key words in bold and complete the sentences.

1 **Approximately** four babies are born every second and two people die, so

_____.

2 **Bootstrapping** is a self-starting process and in business might refer to

_____.

3 **Gatekeepers** are people such as _____
who make decisions about whether or not you can proceed.

4 Most people are worried about the short term but, **strategically**, people should

_____.

5 The computer was a **transformational** technology because it changed
the way we do things such as banking. A similar technology is

_____ because _____

_____.

B. Look at the key words and think of at least one more collocation for each.
Then think of sentences using the key word and one collocation. Practise
your sentences with a partner, checking each other's vocabulary and grammar.

1 assessment (n.)

individual, _____

2 consultants (n.)

business, _____

3 consumers (n.)

sophisticated, _____

4 income (n.)

above-average, _____

5 option (n.)

possible, _____

Before You Listen

A. Read an excerpt from Listening 1 and answer the questions. Then compare
your answers with a partner's.

> In the cities, the divide between rich and poor is stark. But the streets pulse
> with the spirit of hope and change. It's the perfect testing ground for an
> inspiring new wave of entrepreneurship, businesses that blend profit with
> purpose. The story of one of those companies begins in Bogotá at one of
> the biggest, busiest markets in South America. In the midst of the bedlam
> and balancing acts, two dynamic young entrepreneurs are using business
> to change the world, one plantain at a time.

1 Besides money, what else divides the rich and poor?

_____

_____

2 Fair trade coffee production (where coffee growers receive a fair wage) is an example of an industry that blends profit with purpose. What is another example?

_____

_____

3 Predict how you think the young entrepreneurs might change the way traditional food markets operate?

_____

_____

B. Similes can often help you understand and remember key concepts. Think of similes for five of the important ideas in Listening 1.

1 a busy food market is like _____.

2 the distribution of food is like _____.

3 working long hours is like _____.

4 texting food orders is like _____.

5 not owning your own home is like _____.

While You Listen

C. Watch the video once to get the general idea. Watch it again to fill in the blanks. If necessary, watch it a third time to check your answers and add more details.

NOTES
1 Carolina Medina and Verena Liedgens, co-founders of a start-up called Agruppa solving the global food crisis.   Help people get access to food that's _____.
2 Works with mom-and-pop shops in _____.
3 Goal: better prices _____.
4 Street vendors and mom-and-pop shops sell _____ of the food in Colombia.
5 They spend around _____ hours per week and around   _____ of their income only in transportation.
6 They work long hours _____.
7 Shop owners text _____; goods delivered to neighbourhood.
8 They want a _____.

9 Agruppa wants to be an ally of _____.

10 Agora is a non-profit organization in Latin America and the Caribbean that supports _____.

11 Agora assigns a person to your _____.

12 300,000+ mom-and-pops shops: business has unlimited _____.

13 Potential for Agruppa around _____.

14 Cali: In the hillside neighbourhood of Polvorines, dusty _____,

no running _____, homes made of _____.

15 The community = _____ families that don't have formal title for their _____.

16 Up to 75 percent of Colombians live in properties they don't _____.

17 Matt helps people get formal title to the properties they've worked _____.

18 The lack of ownership is perpetuating the _____.

19 With no legal title to their properties, they can't apply for _____.

20 When someone decides to apply for title, the company uses an app for _____.

21 Suyo's lawyers, architects, and engineers go into historical _____ mode.

22 Agora's focused on our region, Latin America, so they understand our _____.

23 Agora Partnerships helps unleash the potential of _____.

24 When it comes to eliminating poverty, ending climate change, and fighting inequality around the globe,

they know we're all in this _____ .

After You Listen

D. The video describes three companies. What does each do?

1 Agora: _____

2 Agruppa: _____

3 Suyo: _____

E. Read the following statements and use what you learned in Focus on Critical Thinking (page 31) to choose the simile that best captures each idea.

1 The Agruppa co-founders met at the London School of Economics.

a) They were like ships passing in the night.

b) They were like strangers in a crowd.

c) They were like birds at the same feeder.

2 Agruppa's main concern is to improve the diets of local people.

   a) Improving local diets is like creating a bigger food bowl.

   b) You can't have your cake and eat it too.

   c) Give people a fish and you feed them for a day.

3 Mom-and-pop shops are mostly found in low-income neighbourhoods because poor people cannot afford to shop once a week.

   a) Buying food is like swimming; if you go too far, you can't get back.

   b) Buying food is like sleeping; if you don't wake up early, you're late.

   c) Buying food is like eating; if you do too much at once, you can be wasteful.

4 Shop owners spend a high percentage of their income on transportation; this suggests their earnings are low.

   a) Spending money on travel can be like throwing money away.

   b) Transportation is all about being as free as a bird.

   c) It's not the destination that matters as much as the journey.

5 Agruppa will likely move from a garage to a warehouse when they expand their network of businesses.

   a) A garage is like a city and a warehouse is like a country.

   b) It's like shoes; as you grow, you need a bigger size.

   c) A network is like a small spiderweb in a big warehouse.

6 The hillside neighbourhood of Los Polvorines is probably home to the poor because no one else wants to live there.

   a) Bad land is like bad food, if you're hungry enough, you'll take what you can get.

   b) A hill is like a wall; you cannot climb it without the right equipment.

   c) A neighbourhood is like a bird's nest.

7 The fact that there's no running water in Los Polvorines suggests the government doesn't care as much about the area.

   a) It's like the squeaky wheel gets the grease.

   b) It's like being forgotten by your parents.

   c) It's like the nail that sticks out gets hammered down.

8 An important reason for getting legal title to a property is so owners can leave it to their children.

   a) It's like finding a pot of gold at the end of a rainbow.

   b) It's like stealing from the rich to give to the poor.

   c) It's like passing the torch to the next generation.

F. Imagine you were planning on promoting a project similar to one discussed in Listening 1: something to help develop social entrepreneurs, organize market deliveries, or assist homeowners in securing property rights. Use what you learned in Focus on Listening (page 30) to give a persuasive, one-minute talk to explain the project's importance. Practise with your partner, then present your project in a group.

MyBookshelf > My eLab >
Exercises > Chapter 2 >
Reimagining Business
in Latin America

Talking about Sequencing

Sequencing helps speakers and listeners explain and understand how things happen over time—and in what precise order. The most common way to express a sequence is with words such as *first, second,* and *third*.

This table includes examples of words that signal events at the beginning, middle, and end of a sequence, as well as things that sometimes happen.

BEGINNING	MIDDLE	SOMETIMES	END
• at first	• after	• from time to time	• eventually
• first of all	• at this point	• gradually	• finally
• in the beginning	• during this time	• occasionally	• in the end
• initially	• later	• seldom	• last
• to begin with	• meanwhile	• some of the time	• ultimately
• to start with	• next		• when it was over
	• then		

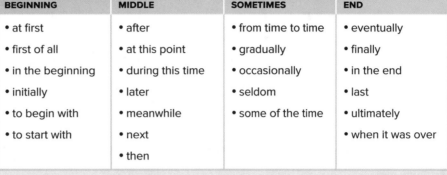

A. Read an excerpt adapted from Listening 3 and highlight all the sequence words.

> To begin with, Yunus tried to persuade his local bank to lend money to the poor. He explained the situation; the bank said that the poor are not creditworthy. After several months, he offered to become a guarantor for the loans to the poor. Later, he was stunned by the results; gradually, all the poor paid back their loans. Occasionally, he would try to expand the program through existing banks but when rejected, he decided to create a separate bank for the poor. He finally succeeded in doing that in 1983: Grameen Bank (Village Bank).

B. One challenge is to understand a sequence when a speaker goes back and forth in time. Besides the words in the table above, consider how other words help establish time. Number the sentences adapted from Listening 2 in the most logical order.

____1____ Thelma has lived in Silicon Valley since 1959.

_____ Eventually, they found a novel way to keep in contact with their grandmother: a robot with a communication tablet.

_____ Later, she got used to the new technology.

_____ A year ago, Thelma started living in an apartment in a nursing home.

_____ After she moved to the nursing home, her kids and grandchildren weren't able to visit her often.

_____ Before that, she was living in a house.

_____ To start with, Thelma wasn't sure about the robot.

____8____ Now it's her best friend.

C. Think about a sequence of events that happened, such as how you spent a day on the weekend. Use at least eight sequence words, two from each column in the table above. Share your sequence with a partner and then in a group.

MyBookshelf > My eLab > Exercises > Chapter 2 > Accuracy Review

How much of a company's success is based on the attitudes of its founders? Young people who start businesses today are less likely to follow the same approaches as those who came before them. This is particularly true of start-ups that are looking for ways to improve people's lives.

VOCABULARY BUILD

In the following exercises, explore key words from Listening 2.

A. Many words have noun, verb, adjective, and adverb forms. Fill in the chart with the missing forms. Key words are in black. After, write a short definition for each key word.

NOUN	VERB	ADJECTIVE	ADVERB	DEFINITION
❶ *ultimatum*			ultimately	
❷		disruptive		
❸ diversity				
❹ investor				
❺			presumably	

B. For each key word in bold, choose the one item that does not fit. Then practise using each key word in a sentence with a partner.

  ❶ **colleagues** (n.) friends, bosses, employees, supervisors

  ❷ **perspective** (n.) viewpoint, outlook, opinion, suggestion

  ❸ **retain** (v.) keep, discard, preserve, maintain

  ❹ **revenue** (n.) earnings, profit, costs, income

  ❺ **watershed** (n.) breakpoint, turning point, achievement, loss

C. Write a sentence containing each of these pairs of words.

  ❶ perspective / ultimately

  _____

  _____

  ❷ diversity / investor

  _____

  _____

  ❸ watershed / presumably

  _____

  _____

Before You Listen

A. Read an excerpt from Listening 2 and answer the questions.

> So as we look to the future, we've had waves of technological disruption, the last two being social and mobile. What's the next disruption, social disruption? Any idea?

1 What is the greatest technological disruption you have seen in your lifetime?

_____

_____

2 What is an example of a social disruption?

_____

_____

3 What is an example of a mobile disruption?

_____

_____

B. Listening 2 is divided into two parts. In the first part, the host interviews three entrepreneurs who are interested in how start-ups can help foster change and improve people's lives. The second part is about a home robot that assists a grandmother in communicating with her family. Read about the three entrepreneurs below. With a partner, think of two questions you might ask each one about his or her business.

1 Joshua Landy is an intensive care doctor and co-founder of **Figure 1**, which offers free access to medical images for doctors to share and discuss in order to improve their knowledge.

2 Michael Katchen is the founder and CEO of **Wealthsimple**, which provides free or affordable investment advice. The company also has a social investing portfolio that offers options for investing in good causes.

3 Mallorie Brodie is the CEO and co-founder of **Bridgit**, an app to help the construction industry manage projects more efficiently.

While You Listen

C. Listen to the first part once to get the general idea. While you listen, check if your questions in task B were answered. Then read the interview segments and key point choices on the next page and listen again; choose the key point (*A* or *B*) that best corresponds to each segment.

INTERVIEWS	KEY POINTS: CHOOSE A OR B
1 According to Google Canada, outside Silicon Valley, the Toronto-Waterloo corridor represents the highest concentration of start-ups on the planet.	A: Canada is a disruptive force in terms of innovation. B: Canada is trying to become bigger than Silicon Valley.
2 Joshua Landy: I think it really depends on where that start-up is and who started it.	A: Canada is similar to most other countries in terms of its start-up culture. B: Canada is different in terms of its focus on diversity and equality in the workplace.
3 Host: Michael, you moved back to Toronto from San Francisco to start Wealthsimple. Why did you come home?	A: He lost his job and decided that he would have to try starting over in a less expensive place. B: Friends were returning to Canada and there was government support.
4 Host: We often look at the States because it does have ten times the population and presumably ten times the number of people willing to invest. Do you find the investment culture here in Canada—	A: You need talent, capital, and a market, and Canada supplied them. B: You need time, money, and a capital city, and Toronto qualified as one of them.
5 Michael Katchen: But on the capital side, you know, huge amounts of new capital investing ...	A: There is a problem with start-ups in the Mexican beer market not wanting to work in Canada. B: Canadians don't put business ingredients together to win.
6 Host: Mallorie Brodie, what are you thinking? What hurdles do Canadian start-ups face?	A: You don't have to actually be in the US to make sales in the US. B: You can start in Canada and then quickly open an office in the US.
7 Host: Are there changes you'd like to see that would help grow this sector, Mallorie?	A: We need to improve recruitment to bring talented employees to Canada. B: We need the largest companies in the US to consider coming to work in Canada.
8 Host: So what do you mean when you talk about talent?	A: We need a million to ten million talented people to work in new technology companies. B: We need talented people from other technology companies who can help scale the company up.
9 Host: So when we hear tech company executives talking about the need for visas to be opened up for foreign workers, that's what we're talking about?	A: We need visas, so our best talented scientists can work anywhere in the world using artificial intelligence. B: We need the best talent in artificial intelligence, machine learning, quantum computing, health care, and sciences.
10 Host: So as we look to the future, we've had waves of technological disruption, the last two being social and mobile. What's the next disruption, social disruption? Any idea?	A: Mobile disruptions have not ended, particularly in the financial sector. B: Social disruptions are coming in terms of investing in new competition spaces.
11 Host: Josh Landy, what's the technology most likely to disrupt health care?	A: Hospitals are likely to increase their computing power more than five times. B: Mobile phones will be able to use apps and websites to deliver services.
12 Host: Mallorie, what are you thinking? What's the technology most likely to disrupt the construction industry then?	A: Mobile apps will allow large teams to communicate and work together. B: iPads will become more popular to allow everyone to do their work anywhere.

D. Now listen to the second part about a home robot that connects families. OhmniLabs hopes that this technology will be a disruptor in eldercare. While you listen, complete the *who, what, when, where, why*, and *how* questions.

❶ Who: *Thelma Ackley and her family*

❷ What: _____

_____

❸ When: *Not mentioned*

❹ Where: *Thelma's home in Palo Alto*

❺ Why: _____

_____

❻ How: _____

_____

After You Listen

E. Based on what you heard in Listening 2, what do the three entrepreneurs have in common? Complete the table with check marks.

	JOSHUA LANDY	MICHAEL KATCHEN	MALLORIE BRODIE
❶ has a start-up	✓		
❷ works with the general public			
❸ works with doctors			
❹ needs skilled workers			
❺ sees room to grow			
❻ moved to Canada from the US			

F. Read the questions and write answers based on what you heard in Listening 2.

❶ The term *disruption* is used to describe a new business that changes how things are done. What is an example of a business disruption?

_____

❷ What is an example of cultural DNA?

_____

❸ What is an example of a watershed moment?

_____

❹ What are three key components needed for a successful business?

_____

⑤ Which of the three companies is likely doing the most social good?

_____

⑥ What is the purpose of the OhmniLabs home robot in terms of providing eldercare?

_____

⑦ How might the robot help older people become less dependent on hospitals and rest homes?

_____

_____

⑧ Why might these robots make older people feel less lonely?

_____

_____

MyBookshelf > My eLab >
Exercises > Chapter 2 >
Capitalism on Steroids

G. Many modern social disruptions, like home robots, have the potential to make a lot of money for their start-up owners. Are owner profits justified, or should inventors and others be more concerned with helping others and not just with becoming rich? Why? In a group, discuss the points for and against each side and consider how profit encourages people to be more innovative.

WARM-UP ASSIGNMENT
Prepare an Elevator Pitch to Explain a Good Cause

The term *elevator pitch* refers to selling an idea to an investor in the few minutes it takes an elevator to go from a building's lobby to its top floor. Create a two-minute elevator pitch that identifies a social problem in the developing world; use what you learned in Focus on Listening (page 30) to persuade your listeners about its importance.

A. Choose a topic related to an issue discussed in this chapter:
  • Access to clean water
  • Access to education
  • Access to food
  • Access to medical care
  • Access to shelter
  • Access to work opportunities

Visit *My eLab Documents for referencing guidelines for APA, MLA, and IEEE citation styles.*

B. Research the problem online (other than on *Wikipedia*) and in the library. Keep a record of your sources, following the citation style preferred in your field of study.

C. Structure your elevator pitch on a separate page. Follow the steps on the opposite page to explain the problem and give general background information. Write notes relating to your topic in the right-hand column.

STEPS	NOTES
1 Ask a rhetorical question that presents the problem to your audience. A rhetorical question is used to make a point or get the audience to think, rather than to elicit a reply. • When you get a glass of water from the tap, do you ever think how miraculous running water would seem to some people in the developing world?	
2 Outline the problem. • Since [date], [large number] people have died because of ... • One key problem that keeps people in poverty is ... • The problem of (...) is most severe in [specific region or country] ...	
3 Use what you learned in Focus on Critical Thinking (page 31) to create a metaphor or simile about the issue. • Denying education to young children is like burning a bridge. • Not having access to jobs is the same as ... • A lack of medical care is a death sentence.	
4 Explain why the issue is so important. • Without help, people will suffer. • No one else is worried about their future. • Something has to be done to make it stop.	

Use feedback from your teacher and classmates on this Warm-Up Assignment to improve your speaking skills.

D. Practise your elevator pitch with a partner using what you learned in Focus on Listening (page 30) about persuasive speech. Do not read from your page. The speech should be short enough that you only need one cue card for your points.

E. Keep your notes for use in the Final Assignment.

FOCUS ON SPEAKING

Adapting to Changes in Conversations

In a conversation, at some point either you or the other speaker might want to change the topic. But one of you may feel that you aren't finished making your points and want to continue on the topic. Review the following strategies to adapt to changes in conversation.

CHANGE STRATEGIES	PURPOSE	EXAMPLES
INTRODUCING A TOPIC	This can happen at the beginning of a conversation or part way through.	• Something I'd like to discuss is ... • An issue I've been thinking about is ... • We should talk about ...

CHANGE STRATEGIES	PURPOSE	EXAMPLES
AVOIDING A TOPIC	Sometimes you don't wish to, or aren't prepared to, discuss a topic.	• I'd rather not discuss that now. • Could we discuss this later? • I'm not ready to talk about this right now.
RESERVING TIME TO MAKE YOUR POINTS	Sometimes another speaker talks at length and does not leave others a chance to share their ideas. You can make a brief interruption to explain you want time to respond.	• I'd like to talk about (that last point) when you're finished. • When you're done with this point, I'd like to say something about it.
CHANGING A TOPIC	Change a topic when you have nothing more to add and want to end a conversation or start another one.	• On another topic, … • Something else we should discuss is … • Let's move on and talk about …
ACCEPTING A CHANGE IN TOPIC	When someone else suggests changing the topic, you can indicate your agreement.	• Non-verbal nod • Okay. So, what's next? • Fine. Is there something else you'd like to discuss?
AVOIDING A CHANGE OF TOPIC	Another speaker might want to change the topic before you're ready to move on.	• Let's just stick to the topic for a moment. • I have a few points to add before we move on.
RETURNING TO A TOPIC	Sometimes, you want to return to a topic later in a conversation.	• If we can go back to something we discussed earlier, … • I just remembered we should discuss …

A. With a partner, discuss one of the following statements. Continue speaking until you have used each of the change strategies in the above table.

- Everyone should have a digital record of their health, from cradle to grave.
- Everyone should be taught about finances from an early age.
- Just as businesses manage projects, people should have tools to manage their lives.

B. Read each sentence and choose the change strategy you would use to control the conversation.

WHEN THE OTHER PERSON SAYS …	USE THIS CHANGE STRATEGY …
❶ Let's move on. I think I've heard enough about that topic right now.	
❷ I'm sorry, but I'm not quite sure what we're talking about.	
❸ If you'll just bear with me, it won't take me more than forty-five minutes or an hour to share my ideas.	
❹ I know you've said you didn't want to discuss this, but …	
❺ Sorry for talking for so long. I know you wanted to add something.	

If someone becomes rude or insulting, end the talk.

MyBookshelf > My eLab >
Exercises > Chapter 2 >
Focus on Speaking

Poverty Is a Threat to Peace

Dynamite inventor Alfred Nobel's (1833–1896) wealth from the sale of weapons troubled him. Before his death, he established Nobel Prizes for sciences, literature, and peace. Muhammad Yunus (1940–), a Bangladeshi economics professor, was awarded the Nobel Peace Prize for establishing microcredit loans that have allowed countless people to rise out of poverty.

VOCABULARY BUILD

In the following exercises, explore key words from Listening 3.

A. Words can change in meaning depending on the context in which they are used. For each of the following words, write two sentences, each with a different context. After, compare sentences with a partner and look for additional contexts.

① creditworthy

_____

_____

② guarantor

_____

_____

③ cumulative

_____

_____

④ synergy

_____

_____

⑤ foundation

_____

_____

B. Define each of the following words and think of a sentence that helps explain it. Practise your sentences with a partner.

① advocate (v.) _____

② constructs (n.) _____

③ infrastructure (n.) _____

④ interventions (n.) _____

⑤ theoretical (adj.) _____

MyBookshelf > My eLab > Exercises > Chapter 2 > Vocabulary Review

Before You Listen

A. What do you know about microcredit loans—very small loans that give poor people enough capital to start a small business? An example might be a loan to buy a few ducks whose eggs could be sold. Discuss microcredit loans with a partner and how a small sum of money could be used to start a business. What business might you start if you got a small loan?

B. In Focus on Listening (page 30), you learned how certain elements of speech can be used to persuade listeners. Here is an excerpt from Yunus's acceptance speech. Read and discuss it with a partner. What expectations does the introduction create for the listener? What would you expect the rest of the speech to be about?

> [Ladies and gentlemen,] by giving us this prize, the Norwegian Nobel Committee has given important support to the proposition that peace is inextricably linked to poverty. Poverty is a threat to peace.
>
> World income distribution gives a very telling story. Ninety-four percent of the world income goes to 40 percent of the world population, while 60 percent of people live on only 6 percent of world income. Half of the world population lives on two dollars a day.

While You Listen

C. Yunus includes many dates and statistics in his acceptance speech. The first time you listen to the speech, fill in as much of the missing data as you can. Listen a second time to check your answers and add any details that you missed.

YUNUS'S SPEECH

❶ World leaders gathered at the United Nations, in _____, and adopted, among others, a historic goal to reduce poverty by half, by _____.

❷ _____ and the Iraq war, and suddenly the world became derailed from the pursuit of this dream.

❸ Till now, over _____ has been spent on the war in Iraq by the USA alone.

❹ The creation of opportunities for majority of the people—the poor—is at the heart of the work that we have dedicated ourselves, during the past thirty years.

❺ In _____, I found it difficult to teach elegant theories of economics in the university classroom, in the backdrop of a terrible famine that was raging in Bangladesh.

❻ When my list was complete, I had the names of _____ victims who borrowed a total amount of US$ _____.

❼ That was when I decided to create a separate bank for the poor. I finally succeeded in doing that in _____. I named it Grameen Bank or Village Bank.

8 Today, Grameen Bank gives loans to nearly _____ million poor people; _____ of them are women. In _____ villages of Bangladesh, Grameen Bank gives collateral-free income-generating loans ...

9 Since it introduced them in _____, housing loans have become, have been used to construct _____ houses.

10 In a cumulative way, the bank has given out a loan totalling about _____ billion dollars.

11 The repayment rate is _____.

12 Financially, it is self-reliant and has not taken donor money since _____.

13 Deposits and only resources of Grameen Bank today amount to _____ of all outstanding loans.

14 _____ of our borrowers have crossed the poverty line.

15 It is _____ years now since we began.

16 One of the _____ Decisions developed and followed by them are to send children to school.

17 Grameen Bank now gives _____ scholarships every year.

18 There are _____ students on student loans.

19 Over _____ students are added to this number annually.

20 In Bangladesh, _____ of the poor families have been reached with microcredit.

21 We are hoping that by _____, all _____ of the poor families will be reached with microcredit.

22 There are now _____ beggars in the program.

23 About _____ of them have already stopped begging completely.

24 Typical loan to a beggar is only _____.

25 Today, there are nearly _____ telephone ladies providing telephone service in all the villages of Bangladesh.

㉖ Grameen Phone has more than _____ subscribers, and is the largest mobile phone company in the country.

㉗ ... the telephone ladies, they generate _____ of the revenue of the company.

㉘ Out of the _____ board members who are present here today, _____ are telephone ladies.

㉙ Telenor owns _____ share of the company; Grameen Telecom owns _____.

㉚ The country with the richest and freest market fails to provide health care for _____ of its population.

㉛ Social business is important because it addresses very vital concerns of mankind. It can change the lives

of the bottom _____ of the world population and help them to get out of poverty.

㉜ Each hospital will undertake _____ cataract surgeries per year at differentiated prices to the rich and the poor.

After You Listen

D. With a partner, discuss one of the following statements. Continue speaking until you have used each of the change strategies from Focus on Speaking (page 43).

- People in poverty cannot get ahead because they cannot escape debt.
- It is far better to invest in businesses run by women.
- The world is not doing enough to understand and overcome poverty.

E. Decide if each statement is true or false. For each false statement, write a true one.

STATEMENTS	TRUE	FALSE
❶ Yunus believes that there is a link between overcoming poverty and achieving peace. _____ _____		
❷ Yunus says that everyone in the world should be earning the same amount. _____ _____		
❸ Yunus feels that there are social, political, and economic perspectives to achieving peace. _____ _____		
❹ Yunus blames human rights for the spread of poverty in the developing world. _____ _____		

STATEMENTS	TRUE	FALSE
5 Yunus became involved in poverty issues because he was a policy-maker and a researcher. _____ _____		
6 Yunus compares moneylending practices to recruiting slave labour. _____ _____		
7 When Yunus approached his campus bank, they were happy to provide loans to the poor. _____ _____		
8 The name Grameen Bank was probably chosen to focus on the importance of village life. _____ _____		
9 The idea of providing loans to women was to enhance the benefits to their families. _____ _____		
10 Yunus suggests that we have many assumptions that overestimate human capacity. _____ _____		

F. Listening 3 features an extended metaphor around poor people and bonsai. However, Yunus is mistaken about bonsai; the plants are miniature because key roots are clipped, not because of poor soil. It's important to be precise in your metaphors. What is the meaning of the following wealth-related metaphors? Which are similar, and which are quite different? Discuss in a group.

- Money doesn't grow on trees.
- The rich get richer; the poor get poorer.
- Money doesn't buy you happiness.
- Money isn't everything.
- Money makes money.
- Put your money where your mouth is.
- Poverty is no crime.

MyBookshelf > My eLab >
Exercises > Chapter 2 >
Poverty Is a Threat to Peace

Academic
Survival Skill

Working with Statistics

Statistics can add weight to a presentation or discussion. But how often have you listened to a speech full of numbers and come away confused or unable to remember the details? When using statistics in a speech, it's important to present the numerical data in a clear and relevant way that has the maximum impact on your audience.

A. You can present numerical data in different ways, for example with fractions (1/5), percentages (20 percent), or written expressions (one in five). The choice can affect your audience's perception of the significance of the number. Fill in the missing figures and words in the following table.

FRACTION	PERCENTAGE	WRITTEN EXPRESSIONS
1/5	20 percent	one-fifth one in five
1/4		
1/3		
1/2		
2/3		
3/4		
97/100		almost all …

B. Statistics can often seem boring and meaningless. Consider these figures:

> Canada's rate of relative child poverty is **14** percent, which ranks the country twenty-fourth of thirty-five industrialized countries (UNICEF, 2016).

UNICEF Canada (2016). *Report card 10*. Retrieved from https://www.unicef.ca/en/our-work/article/unicef-report-card-10

Now look at the same information presented in a more forceful way.

> What do these industrialized countries have in common? Luxembourg, United Kingdom, Estonia, New Zealand, Slovakia, Australia, Hungary, Belgium, Malta, France, Germany, Ireland, Switzerland, Czech Republic, Austria, Sweden, Denmark, Slovenia, Norway, Netherlands, Cyprus, Finland, Iceland. Here's the answer: in every single one of them, children are better off than they are in Canada. Fourteen percent of children in Canada—that's one in seven children—are living in poverty. We can do better.

The rhetorical question at the beginning of the paragraph prompts you to reflect, and the list of countries is like a riddle that you have to solve. Even though you cannot be expected to remember the names of all the countries, you are left with a strong impression that Canada is far below international standards.

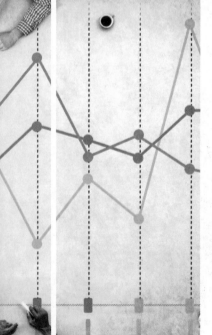

C. Read the following statement and edit it to make it more memorable. Then share it with a partner.

> On average across OECD countries, 13.5 percent of children live in income poverty, but rates do differ considerably from country to country. In five OECD countries (Chile, Israel, Spain, Turkey, and the United States) more than 20 percent of children live in poverty, with rates particularly high—at around 25 percent—in Israel and Turkey. In Denmark and Finland, the child income poverty rate is only around 3–4 percent. (Adapted from OECD, 2017)
>
> OECD. (2017). *Child poverty*. OECD Family Database. Social Policy Division, Directorate of Employment, Labour and Social Affairs. Retrieved from http://www.oecd.org/els/family/database.htm

D. It is often difficult for people to comprehend numbers without comparing them to more easily imaginable times or quantities. Consider the following statistics on the earnings of the wealthiest and poorest people in the world.

> In 2016, the International Monetary Fund estimated that the average income of a person living in Qatar was US$129,726. The average income of a person living in the Central African Republic was US$656.
>
> Gregson, J. (2017, February 13) The world's richest and poorest countries. *Global Finance*. Retrieved from https://www.gfmag.com/global-data/economic-data/worlds-richest-and-poorest-countries

The same information can be expressed in this way:

> On average, a worker in the Central African Republic would have to work more than 197 years to earn the same yearly income as a person living in Qatar.

With a partner, discuss which presentation is more effective and why.

E. Now read the following excerpt from Yunus's speech. Think of a way to express the statistics so that they are more memorable, for example, by comparing the cost of a typical loan to what you might normally spend twelve dollars on. Rewrite the excerpt on a separate page.

> Three years ago, we started an exclusive program focusing on the beggars. None of Grameen Bank's rules apply to them. Loans are interest free; they can pay whatever amount they wish, whenever they wish. We gave them the idea to carry small merchandise such as snacks, toys for the kids or household items for the housewives, when they went from house to house for begging. The idea worked. There are now 85,000 beggars in the program. About 5000 of them have already stopped begging completely. Typical loan to a beggar is $12.

© **ERPI** • Reproduction prohibited

FINAL ASSIGNMENT

Deliver an Appeal for Support

Now it's your turn. Use everything you have learned in this chapter to research and deliver an appeal for support on the elevator pitch you created in the Warm-Up Assignment (page 42).

A. Review your Warm-Up Assignment with your partner and use what you learned in Academic Survival Skill (page 50) to find statistics that support the cause you identified. Be sure to convert the statistics into meaningful ideas, perhaps drawing on what you learned in Focus on Critical Thinking (page 31) about metaphors and/or similes. Remember to properly cite and reference your sources.

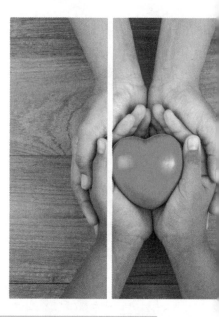

B. Plan your presentation. Use the table to organize your notes. As you prepare, imagine that each member of the group you are talking to has $10,000 to support your ideas. Use what you learned in Focus on Listening (page 30) to make a persuasive appeal so they will agree to donate to your cause.

PRESENTATION STRUCTURE	NOTES
1 Outline the problem or challenges in detail. Use what you learned in Focus on Accuracy (page 37) to explain the sequence of how the problem developed over time.	
2 Cite statistics, but look for ways to make the numbers more meaningful to your listeners, such as using metaphors or similes.	
3 Provide one or more possible solutions that require an investment from sponsors.	
4 Make a personal appeal. Ask your listeners to consider the needs of your cause. Appeal to the listeners' emotions.	
5 Thank your potential sponsors and allow time for questions. Be sure to have references on hand to support your facts and statistics in case you are asked.	

C. Form groups of six or more students. Remember that each of you has $10,000 to award to the group with the best presentation—but you cannot give the money to your own group! Give your presentation and answer questions about it. Use the change strategies you learned in Focus on Speaking (page 43) to manage the conversation. Ask other groups about their presentations.

D. After all the pairs of partners have finished speaking, decide to which pair you will donate your $10,000. After, review your presentation and discussion and reflect on what you could improve next time.

Critical Connections

Not all aid and innovation projects end happily. Ghanaian economist Dr. George Ayittey has described international aid in Africa using a quotation commonly attributed to Albert Einstein (1879–1955): "Insanity is defined as doing the same thing over and over again and expecting different results."

A. Consider the following case study:

In the 1980s, Norway built a fish processing plant on the shores of Lake Turkana, Kenya, to help economically disadvantaged local tribespeople who suffer during frequent droughts. However, the local people are nomadic livestock herders. The multi-million-dollar plant today sits vacant.

B. In a group, discuss the following questions.

1. What should Norway have done before spending millions of dollars building the fish plant?

2. What new use could the fish plant be put to now?

3. What new project might help the Turkana tribespeople in the future?

4. What metaphor or simile could you use for one aspect of this story?

As you discuss your ideas on the issues, use what you learned in Focus on Speaking (page 43) to manage the conversation.

Loiyangalani Village, Lake Turkana, Kenya

CHAPTER 3

Private Eyes

Is your personal data being collected, used, and/or abused? The answer is certainly *yes*. Increasingly, new technologies and powerful computer programs are being deployed along with your digital footprint to uncover as much as possible about you. It starts when you shop or use social media online, or step out the door and are caught on video cameras set up by businesses or traffic authorities. Street cameras often use facial recognition to determine your identity based on other online records. Although the purpose is to catch criminals, businesses employ the same technologies to identify customers. How much does privacy mean to you?

In this chapter, you will

- learn vocabulary related to privacy and digital devices;

- listen to infer attitudes;

- identify pros and cons;

- express beliefs, facts, and opinions accurately;

- use Likert scales to measure attitudes;

- examine methods to provide counterarguments;

- conduct a survey on a privacy topic and discuss the results in a group.

GEARING UP

A. Look at the infographic and answer the questions.

① *Hacking* refers to gaining unauthorized access to or destroying others' digital information. People who engage in this activity are called *hackers*; what motivates them?

_____

_____

② A Trojan horse virus is often downloaded as part of another program. Why are people not more careful about what they download?

_____

_____

③ *Phishing* uses people's willingness to share their private information without thinking of the consequences. Why do people give up information such as passwords to strangers?

_____

_____

④ Scams often involve offering people love or money to get their bank information and conduct illegal transfers. Why might people not report these scams when they fall for them?

_____

_____

B. Compare your answers, first with a partner, then in a group. Choose the best answers.

Below are the key words you will practise in this chapter. Check the words you understand then underline the words you use. Highlight the words you need to learn.

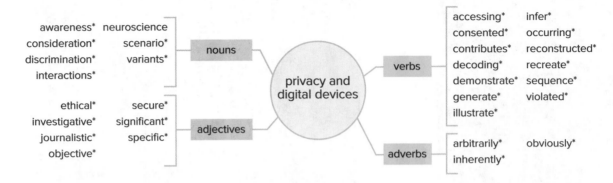

nouns

awareness* neuroscience
consideration* scenario*
discrimination* variants*
interactions*

adjectives

ethical* secure*
investigative* significant*
journalistic* specific*
objective*

privacy and digital devices

verbs

accessing* infer*
consented* occurring*
contributes* reconstructed*
decoding* recreate*
demonstrate* sequence*
generate* violated*
illustrate*

adverbs

arbitrarily* obviously*
inherently*

*Appears on the Academic Word List

© ERPI • Reproduction prohibited

Inferring Attitudes

When you listen, you pay attention to the words people use, the way they put those words together in sentences, and the attitude(s) the words convey. Attitude refers to how speakers feel about what they are saying: positive, negative, or neutral. In some cases, speakers can express these three attitudes in one sentence.

A. One way for speakers to express their attitude is through the use of adjectives and adverbs. Read the following sentences adapted from Listening 1 and decide whether the message is positive, negative, or neutral based on what is said and the words in bold.

SENTENCES	POSITIVE	NEGATIVE	NEUTRAL
1 But there are also concerns that these vast databases pose a **significant** risk to our privacy.			
2 Now, in this **particular** test, people are given photographs of just the eye region.			
3 As you can imagine, everyone is **perfectly** good at this.			
4 So we get a small fraction of the total genome but the information that's contained is **tremendous**.			
5 I've seen papers where faces are reconstructed based on genomic data from, for example, 23andMe data sets that are **eerily** close to the actual person.			
6 It's fair to have a **reasonable** degree of faith.			

▶

B. Attitudes can also be expressed by applying different stress patterns to words in a sentence or by changing the tone, for example by turning a statement into a question. With a partner, read the following sentences aloud. How does phrasing the words as a statement or a question affect your impression of the speaker's attitude? Which one expresses more certainty, and which one more doubt?

• It's fair to have a reasonable degree of faith.

• It's fair to have a reasonable degree of faith?

C. Try reading the sentences above again, stressing one word more than others. How does this seem to change the speaker's attitude?

D. Read the paragraph from Listening 3. What is the speaker's attitude toward the topic? List three adjectives or adverbs that convey this attitude.

ATTITUDE: ☐ POSITIVE ☐ NEGATIVE ☐ NEUTRAL

ADJECTIVES AND ADVERBS: _____

> I think there is a very high level of vulnerability. The reason is that you don't have to actually pick up entire thoughts. There are signals that our brains make when we see something that we recognize or we see something that's unexpected. And these are very specific shape waveforms that can be detected. So if the electrodes or the recording devices are accurate enough and the processing is available, you can detect these things. And this leads to an opportunity to interact with a person to extract information.

FOCUS ON CRITICAL THINKING

Identifying Pros and Cons

When you are faced with a difficult decision, it helps to consider the pros (points in favour) and cons (points against). Although you may have the same number of pros as cons, one pro may override a dozen cons. For example, points in favour of gambling may include fun and social opportunities, but a single con—the threat of debt—may outweigh both of these.

A. Read two excerpts from Listening 1. Highlight the pros and underline the cons. Compare your answers with a partner.

> So, these huge databases like 23andMe are extremely valuable for researchers such as Mr. Warrier and they should be very useful for identifying the genetic roots of disease—from mental disorders like autism, schizophrenia, and dementia, to things like heart disease, or even cancer.
>
> I think it's fair to have a reasonable degree of faith that companies like 23andMe are doing a decent job. I think it's important though not to think that it's completely safe. Every little bit of information about you that is revealed can potentially be correlated with third-party data sources to start to chip away at your privacy. And it's important to recognize those dangers.

B. Pros and cons are often presented to support opinions. Read the following three sentences. With a partner, decide whether each one presents a pro or a con. Try to identify the speaker's motivation in each sentence. For example, what language and examples does the speaker use to persuade listeners?

1 We carry our phones like we're married to them and we don't really realize how much information we're giving away to companies when we download smartphone apps.

☐ PRO   ☐ CON

MOTIVATION: _____

_____

2 You're part of an exclusive group that is going to get a sneak peek at our daily horoscope app.

☐ PRO   ☐ CON

MOTIVATION: _____

_____

3 Along with the latest in robots and entertainment systems, an entire industry is springing up now that's aimed at giving you back some personal power.

☐ PRO   ☐ CON

MOTIVATION: _____

_____

C. Consider something you would like to do and your motivation for doing it. In a group, discuss the pros of the action and try to persuade your group members. Your group members identify the cons and try to persuade you that it's not a good idea.

LISTENING 1   **Is Your Genetic Privacy Safe?**

Do you know a secret code? Perhaps not, but your body does. DNA (deoxyribonucleic acid) is the coded information that determines a lot about who you are—from your ethnicity, to diseases you might suffer from, to how empathetic you are. Would you share that information with others?

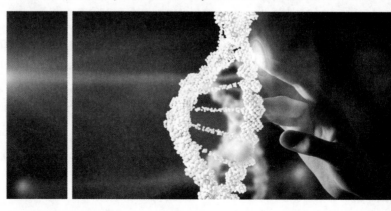

| VOCABULARY BUILD | In the following exercises, explore key words from Listening 1. |

A. Match each key word to the word that forms a collocation with it. Then, with a partner, take turns using each collocation in a sentence.

KEY WORDS		WORDS THAT FORM COLLOCATIONS
❶ contributes	_____	a) statistically
❷ discrimination	_____	b) logical
❸ scenario	_____	c) racial
❹ sequence	_____	d) financially
❺ significant	_____	e) doomsday

B. Read the key words below and write a definition for each one. Then have a short conversation with a partner, using the key words. For example, you may begin with, "Have you ever *consented* to someone else using one of your passwords?" Continue until you have used all the words.

❶ consented _____

❷ consideration _____

❸ inherently _____

❹ reconstructed _____

❺ variants _____

C. Listening 1 includes some technical language about genetics, the study of heredity. With a partner, match the terms with their meanings; look up any you don't know.

TERMS		MEANINGS
❶ anonymize data	_____	a) material that carries the genetic information of living organisms
❷ cognitive traits	_____	b) discovering the properties of a set of genes
❸ DNA	_____	c) the complete set of genes in a cell or organism
❹ genome	_____	d) make it impossible for others to identify an individual from collected information
❺ genome sequencing	_____	e) visible characteristics that relate to a genotype
❻ phenotypes	_____	f) aspects of thinking processes

Before You Listen

A. Read an excerpt from Listening 1. What are the pros and cons of the 23andMe database?

> As more and more people get their genomes scanned, huge genetic databases can be assembled. And these become a fantastic resource for scientists both inside and outside these companies to study. More than sixty research papers have been published using genetic information garnered from the 23andMe database. This kind of data is exactly what scientists need to identify the roots of complex diseases and disorders. But there are also concerns that these vast databases pose a significant risk to our privacy—and that we don't really understand what we're doing when we give private companies—or any organization—control of our genetic information.

PROS: _____

_____

CONS: _____

_____

While You Listen

B. Listen carefully for the interview points below; the questions have been omitted. Listen again to identify the pros and/or cons that are presented for each point. Listen a third time to add information about the speaker's attitude: *positive, neutral, negative,* or *divided* between positive and negative.

INTERVIEW POINTS	PROS AND CONS
1 23andMe, one of a number of groups that in recent years have been selling a new kind of service …	PROS/CONS: *tell you about your ancestry and risk for disease* ATTITUDE: *positive*
2 But this isn't all about you. As more and more people get their genomes scanned, …	PROS/CONS: ATTITUDE:
3 More than sixty research papers have been published using genetic information …	PROS/CONS: ATTITUDE: *divided*
4 Varun Warrier is one of the researchers who has been able to use the 23andMe data in his work …	PROS/CONS: ATTITUDE:
5 We were interested in a whole bunch of cognitive traits that contribute to …	PROS/CONS: ATTITUDE:
6 We wanted to look at the genetic variants in your genome that contribute to …	PROS/CONS: ATTITUDE:
7 Since 23andMe has got privacy and legal clauses, they can't share …	PROS/CONS: ATTITUDE:

INTERVIEW POINTS	PROS AND CONS
8 Yes, so what happened, I think close to 90,000 customers from 23andMe ...	PROS/CONS: ATTITUDE:
9 We found that approximately a third of the total variants in performance ...	PROS/CONS: ATTITUDE:
10 What we were able to identify was	PROS/CONS: ATTITUDE:
11 So, these huge databases like 23andMe are extremely valuable for researchers ...	PROS/CONS: ATTITUDE:
12 But some researchers think you should know that there are privacy risks ...	PROS/CONS: ATTITUDE:
13 I would say extremely valuable. ...	PROS/CONS: ATTITUDE:
14 Well, for example, I've seen some interesting papers, where things like ...	PROS/CONS: ATTITUDE:
15 Very true. That's absolutely true. I think the consideration should be that you know.	PROS/CONS: ATTITUDE:
16 Now we do have a law being passed ...	PROS/CONS: ATTITUDE:
17 Indeed. And those laws ... We have a similar law in the United States. They're ...	PROS/CONS: ATTITUDE:
18 Now 23andMe does make efforts to anonymize their data.	PROS/CONS: ATTITUDE:
19 I think it's fair to have a reasonable degree of faith that companies like 23andMe are doing a decent job.	PROS/CONS: ATTITUDE:
20 It's a danger. It's a danger and that makes re-identification of subjects ...	PROS/CONS: ATTITUDE:
21 Right, so for example, if you posted on Facebook that you had ...	PROS/CONS: ATTITUDE:

After You Listen

C. Sometimes, an individual's personal medical information might benefit a whole group. After listening to the interview, what do you think is generally more important: the individual's right to privacy, or the public's right to medical information that might help save lives?

_____

_____

D. Based on what you can infer from Listening 1, answer the following questions. After, check your answers with a partner and see if you agree.

1 Why might companies such as 23andMe be considered controversial?

_____

_____

2 As a science student, why might Varun Warrier be less concerned about genetic data privacy?

_____

_____

3 What is a possible practical application of understanding someone's level of empathy?

_____

_____

4 Warrier's research shows that genetics might control _part_ of a trait. What other factors might control, for example, a person's intelligence?

_____

_____

5 Why might you decide that posting your genetic information on Facebook is a bad idea?

_____

_____

E. Based on what you learned in Listening 1, answer the questions and then discuss your answers with a partner.

1 Would you get your DNA sequenced? Why or why not?

_____

2 Would you share your DNA results to help further medical research? Why or why not?

_____

3 Would you worry about privacy if your DNA showed you might inherit a dangerous disease? Why or why not?

_____

MyBookshelf > My eLab >
Exercises > Chapter 3 >
Is Your Genetic Privacy Safe?

Expressing Beliefs, Facts, and Opinions

Do you think the number thirteen is unlucky? If so, that's your *belief*. Do you think that some people are superstitious? That is a *fact*; it's true and can't be argued. Do you think that people who are superstitious are silly? That's your *opinion*. We use adverbs and modals to talk about beliefs, facts, and opinions in different ways.

- **Beliefs** are things that are accepted as true by some people even though they can't always be proven.

- **Facts** are things that can be proven or that most people believe are true. Without visiting a distant star, we can use scientific theories to prove that it is hot.

- **Opinions** indicate how you feel about something; they don't depend on facts.

A. Expressing beliefs and facts tends to rely on direct statements and verbs such as *be*, for example, *Hacking is illegal*. However, certain phrases are also used to signal beliefs and facts. Read the following phrases and underline those that indicate beliefs and facts.

1. <u>It's certain ...</u>
2. As far as I understand ...
3. It seems to me that ...
4. It's well known that ...
5. I believe ...

6. Personally, I think ...
7. The fact is ...
8. In my opinion, ...
9. The point is ...
10. There is no doubt ...

B. The phrases in task A that you did not underline indicate opinions. Read the following opinions and highlight the adverbs. Then, work with a partner and take turns using the modals in parentheses to express the same ideas.

1. (could) Apparently, it's easy to listen to others' phone conversations.

   _____

2. (may) Perhaps it's hard to find the special equipment to do so.

   _____

3. (might) If reporters want a story badly enough, maybe that's what they do.

   _____

4. (might) But they could possibly go to jail.

   _____

5. (must) Apparently, the police think it's a big deal.

   _____

6. (must) Anyway, it's certainly a terrible way to collect news.

   _____

C. Decide if each of the following sentences expresses a belief, a fact, or an opinion. After, highlight the modals.

SENTENCES	BELIEF	FACT	OPINION
1 I think there is a very high level of vulnerability.			
2 I should say I'm sounding a bit alarmist here, but I believe that it's very important and part of our mission.			
3 Varun Warrier is a PhD candidate in the department of psychiatry at the University of Cambridge in the United Kingdom.			
4 I would say extremely valuable.			
5 I think it's important, though, not to think that it's completely safe.			

MyBookshelf > My eLab >
Exercises > Chapter 3 >
Accuracy Review

LISTENING ②
VIDEO

Privacy, Consent, and Investigative Journalism

Although you might take some measures to protect your privacy, you probably ignore other things that could affect what information you are sharing, especially related to social media. For instance, how often do you read the terms and conditions that come with software applications?

VOCABULARY BUILD

In the following exercises, explore key words from Listening 2.

A. Many words have noun, verb, adjective, and adverb forms. Fill in the chart with the missing forms. Key words are in black.

NOUN	VERB	ADJECTIVE	ADVERB
1	accessing		
2		investigative	*investigatively**
3		journalistic	*journalistically**
4 objective			
5	illustrate		

* uncommon usage

B. Find a synonym for each key word then write a sentence with the key word.

1 demonstrate (v.) _____

2 secure (adj.) _____

③ ethical (adj.) _____

④ obviously (adv.) _____

⑤ violated (adj.) _____

C. With a partner, read the following sentences and use what you learned in Focus on Critical Thinking (page 57) to think of one or more cons for each pro. Repeat the words in bold in your answers and try to include other key words from this Vocabulary Build.

① Pro: Because of better labelling practices, it's now easy to make **ethical** choices when you shop.

Con: _____

_____

② Pro: Having a key **objective** in your life means you waste less time.

Con: _____

_____

③ Pro: If you use privacy settings on your phone, your data is usually **secure.**

Con: _____

_____

Before You Listen

A. Read an excerpt from Listening 2 and answer the questions. After, discuss your answers with a partner and see if you agree. If possible, try to give examples to support your ideas.

> I need to get your attention. As a journalist, whether I'm writing for online or television, I'm competing against all that clutter out there to try to get you to look at my story. And often, that means journalists have to figure out just how far to push to get you to take notice.

① In your opinion, is it acceptable for journalists to use tricks to get your attention? Why or why not?

_____

_____

_____

② What do you think the speaker means by "all that clutter out there"?

_____

_____

_____

③ What are some ways journalists might "push to get you to take notice"?

_____

_____

_____

B. Listening 2 explores how people don't pay attention to what they are agreeing to when they accept a company's terms and conditions. Which of the following would you accept? Discuss with a partner and share reasons for your answers.

I WOULD GIVE A COMPANY PERMISSION TO	YES	NO
❶ access contact data on my phone		
❷ access my camera		
❸ access my microphone		
❹ read my call logs (records of my phone calls)		
❺ read my text messages		
❻ track my location		

While You Listen

C. Watch once to get the general idea. Watch again to indicate the beliefs and opinions corresponding to the prompts. Watch a third time to check your notes.

SENTENCES	BELIEFS AND OPINIONS
❶ I need to get your attention. As a journalist, …	BELIEFS: *competing against clutter* OPINIONS: *need to push to get attention*
❷ What participants don't know is …	BELIEFS: • people don't care about • they will give away
❸ Shocked by how easy it was for …	BELIEFS: easy for CBC journalists
❹ But not everyone thinks …	OPINIONS: some don't think
❺ You basically broke …	OPINIONS: the speaker's
❻ So did the journalist go too far to illustrate the point?	OPINIONS: can see ethical
❼ So we all live in this app-obsessed world.	BELIEFS: • we are obsessed with • we don't realize how much OPINIONS: people need
❽ And so, you got it to that point and you could've just said to people, "Hey, look what you just agreed to."	OPINIONS: it was interesting to
❾ Like I need to do a better job than skimming.	BELIEFS: needs to do
❿ Okay, so my first thought was, okay, if you just go into someone's phone, they could be …	BELIEFS: they could be in
⓫ So obviously, we had a lot of team discussions. We didn't want to invade …	OPINIONS: • didn't want to invade • it was about

SENTENCES	BELIEFS AND OPINIONS
12 Nothing. And if we would have found it, journalistically, legally, ethically, we wouldn't ...	BELIEFS: *have aired it (shown it on TV)*
13 Yeah, I know, it is, right? Because that's his buddy. He doesn't expect ...	BELIEFS: he doesn't expect
14 Right. So, it is personal information but honestly, I feel like we ...	OPINIONS: *erred on the conservative side*
15 Okay and so we know that ...	BELIEFS:
16 No, not everybody did. But, you know, at the end of the day, big picture, what we were trying to prove ...	BELIEFS: it was
17 We showed them. And I think that's the thing.	OPINIONS: you need to show
18 I'm sure if we would have found anything like that, ...	BELIEFS: it would have been different if
19 And you know, everyone of course is going to talk about, ...	BELIEFS: their devices are
20 I hope so. I mean, one example that I was, you know, using yesterday when talking with someone is, you know, you have your phone now and you can look at a privacy settings page ...	BELIEFS: *phones can display who has access to your data* OPINIONS: *we need something that gives consumers better understanding of what devices are using their information*

After You Listen

D. Check your answers to task A. Do you still feel the same way? Why or why not? Were the journalists' tactics ethical? Discuss with a partner.

E. Read the statements and discuss the questions with a partner. Once you agree on an answer, write it down.

1 The journalists' purpose was to make people aware of privacy abuses. Do you think their approach was effective? For example, would the report make you change your habits? Why or why not?

_____

_____

2 The method was to create an app that offered horoscope information. Do you think the response would be the same if the app was for banking? Why or why not?

_____

_____

3 The journalists were surprised at how little attention people paid to the agreements. Were you surprised? Why or why not?

_____

_____

4 The man who claimed his reading skills were "on point" didn't seem to have read the agreement very carefully. How would you feel seeing this program if you were that man?

_____

_____

5 The point of mentioning Snoop Dodd was to prove that the journalists had hacked the phone. Did this comment go too far? Why or why not?

_____

_____

6 The comment, "It's kind of creepy," likely referred to the idea that others could know so much about you. Are you concerned about information that companies have about you? Why or why not?

_____

_____

7 The comments about the Consumer Trade Show point out that other home devices might be spying on us. Would this make you less likely to buy Internet-connected home devices? Why or why not?

_____

_____

8 The question of whether or not the journalists went too far was probably not part of the original plan for the report. Why might it have been included?

_____

_____

F. How would you feel if you had been picked for the journalists' experiment? Do you think you would have read the agreement materials more carefully? How would you feel after you found out the journalists had accessed your information? In a group, explain why you would or would not have taken part and, if you had, how you would feel after seeing yourself on the program.

MyBookshelf > My eLab >
Exercises > Chapter 3 >
Privacy, Consent, and Investigative
Journalism

Academic
Survival Skill

Measuring Attitudes with Likert Scales

Collecting data is done in various ways, such as through observation and experimentation. Other methods include structured conversations and questionnaires designed to collect data on what people think. One of the most common methods of collecting data about attitudes and opinions is a Likert scale survey.

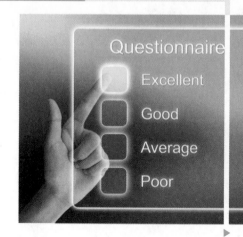

Questionnaire

Excellent

Good

Average

Poor

A Likert scale typically includes five answer points; seven- and nine-point scales are sometimes used, but it can be difficult to understand subtle differences with so many points. Regardless of the choice, the central point indicates a neutral answer. A Likert scale is most often used to measure a response to a statement in terms of agreement, frequency, importance, or likelihood. In the following examples, there is a scale for each item, but it is more common to have a single scale for a series of items.

A. Indicate your response to each of the following items. When you have finished, compare your answers with those of a partner.

AGREEMENT

1 People are concerned about privacy more than ever before.

☐	☐	☐	☐	☐
strongly agree	agree	neither agree nor disagree	disagree	strongly disagree

FREQUENCY

2 I change my technology passwords …

☐	☐	☐	☐	☐
very frequently	frequently	occasionally	seldom	never

IMPORTANCE

3 Maintaining your privacy on social media is …

☐	☐	☐	☐	☐
very important	important	moderately important	of little importance	unimportant

LIKELIHOOD

4 If I am asked by a stranger to share a message online, I will do it.

☐	☐	☐	☐	☐
almost always true	usually true	sometimes true	usually false	almost always false

B. The above Likert scale items are about privacy. Write one more Likert scale item about privacy, fill in the response scale, and ask five students for their responses. Then, in a group, discuss your responses to all the items to see where you agree and disagree.

TYPE OF QUESTION: _____

STATEMENT: _____

☐	☐	☐	☐	☐

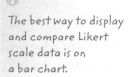

The best way to display and compare Likert scale data is on a bar chart.

WARM-UP ASSIGNMENT
Explore a Topic Related to Privacy

You probably have your own unique attitudes toward privacy. Some people are extremely careful to lock their doors but never change their phone passwords. A few people read software-licensing agreements carefully, while most don't. In this assignment, use what you learned in Academic Survival Skill (page 68) to find out what other students think and do about privacy.

A. This chapter lists several areas where privacy is threatened. Working with a partner, choose one topic to research about privacy. You may choose a new topic or one of the following:

- DNA and medical records
- facial recognition
- government surveillance
- home digital assistants
- Internet-connected devices like dishwashers and shower heads
- passwords
- social media
- software-licensing agreements

B. Brainstorm your topic and think of areas of concern where other students will have different points of view in terms of agreement, frequency, importance, and likelihood.

C. Create a Likert scale survey with statements.

AGREEMENT

① STATEMENT: _____

☐	☐	☐	☐	☐
strongly agree	agree	neither agree nor disagree	disagree	strongly disagree

FREQUENCY

② STATEMENT: _____

☐	☐	☐	☐	☐
very frequently	frequently	occasionally	seldom	never

IMPORTANCE

③ STATEMENT: _____

☐	☐	☐	☐	☐
very important	important	moderately important	of little importance	unimportant

LIKELIHOOD

④ STATEMENT: _____

☐	☐	☐	☐	☐
almost always true	usually true	sometimes true	usually false	almost always false

D. Interview six students using your Likert scale survey. Ask follow-up questions and use what you learned in Focus on Listening (page 56) to infer the students' attitudes.

E. Write summary statements for all of their responses and keep your notes for use in the Final Assignment. Use phrases such as

- Only one student thought ...

- Two of six students believe ...

- All students agree that ...

Use feedback from your teacher and classmates on this Warm-Up Assignment to improve your speaking skills.

LISTENING ❸ Protecting Our Neuroprivacy

It is easy to know when you're excited: your breathing changes, your body becomes tense, and your senses are heightened. But what is your brain doing? Not only can researchers tell that it is active, but they are also learning to translate its electrical signals to discover what you're thinking.

VOCABULARY BUILD

In the following exercises, explore key words from Listening 3.

A. Identify the root word for each of the following key words. Use both the key word and the root word in a sentence. Compare sentences with a partner's and choose the best ones.

KEY WORD	ROOT WORD	SENTENCE
❶ arbitrarily	*arbitrary*	*An arbitrary decision is one that is made without reason, that is, arbitrarily.*
❷ awareness		
❸ decoding		
❹ interactions		
❺ neuroscience		
❻ recreate		

B. Use five of the words in the box to complete the paragraph. Three of the words are not appropriate.

> arbitrarily   generate   infer   interactions   neuroscience
> occurring   recreate   specific

Something that is increasingly _____ is the installation of security cameras on local streets. From this, we can _____ that governments are possibly more nervous about crimes. The installation of these cameras must _____ enormous profits for the companies that manufacture them. Sometimes a _____ home might install its own street cameras, particularly if a crime has been committed nearby. But one finding from _____ is that our perceptions of crime and danger are not always related to facts, so we probably have more cameras than we need.

Before You Listen

A. Read an excerpt from Listening 3 and answer the questions.

> In principle, you can decode any kind of thought that is occurring in the brain at any given point in time. So if we have a suitable brain recording device, we can measure those patterns of activity and infer the relationship between what was going on in your brain and your behaviour or your thought. And you can think about this sort of like writing a dictionary.

1. The phrase *in principle* suggests that the process _____.
   a) is well established
   b) is completely unknown
   c) has a theoretical basis

2. The brain recording device is likely to measure _____.
   a) the weight of the brain
   b) electrical activity
   c) how quickly you think

3. The phrase *writing a dictionary* suggests that _____.
   a) the results are probably true for most people
   b) everyone would have their own dictionary
   c) the brain could interface with word processing

B. Knowing what is going on in your brain would presumably be of interest to many different people. Why might each of the following groups be interested? Write a brief explanation, then discuss your answers in a team.

1. DOCTORS: _____

2. SPORTS COACHES: _____

3. BUSINESS PEOPLE: _____

MyBookshelf > My eLab >
Exercises > Chapter 3 >
Vocabulary Review

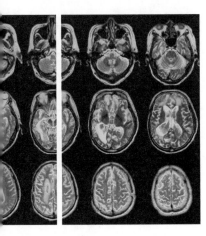

While You Listen

C. Read the questions and the beginnings of the answers. Then listen once to get the general idea. Listen again and take notes to fill in the answers. Listen a third time to check your notes and add details.

1 You have done some work on decoding language and visual images from the brain. Let's start with language. How do you decode words that are happening in the brain?

    1.1 In principle you can decode any kind of thought that _____

        _____

        _____

    1.2 And you can think about this sort of like writing a _____

    1.3 And we essentially play the same game in _____

        _____

    1.4 And by doing that over a very long period of time, we can build up

        _____

        _____

2 How rich is your dictionary at the moment; how much detail can you get?

    2.1 At the moment, we typically generate _____

        _____

3 But you're saying that if I'm watching a movie you would be able to tell from my brain activity whether, what type of movie I was watching—whether it was say, a space movie or a romantic movie or the characters in it? You can see that kind of detail?

    3.1 When you say you can decode this or you can tell what somebody

        is thinking, the question is _____

        _____

        _____

4 So what are your biggest concerns when it comes to things like our neural privacy?

    4.1 As our ability to measure the brain proceeds, our ability to decode the brain will also advance and eventually you will be able to

        _____

        _____

5 When it comes to these consumer brain-computer interface devices, how vulnerable are we and how urgent is this issue?

    5.1 I think there is a very high level of vulnerability. The reason is that

        _____

5.2 So for example, if I showed you in a video game _____

_____

_____

_____

_____

⑥ **Well, how did you test all of this in your laboratory?**

6.1 So we have an EEG system and we put it on _____

_____

6.2 Subliminal images can be put in the game. By monitoring _____

_____

6.3 I have a graduate student who's working on different ways to extract

things like _____

6.4 Let me go back and say an important thing is _____

_____

After You Listen

D. It is now a common crime for people to steal others' personal credit card information, but there are probably no laws against collecting people's thoughts. Are laws needed to protect against this invasion of privacy? Why or why not? Discuss your answers in a small group.

E. Write answers to the following questions, then compare your answers with a partner.

① Say the words *dogs* and *cats* out loud. Do you have a sense that the mention of dogs and cats causes different patterns of activity in your brain? Explain.

_____

_____

② The research shows that information can be collected while people watch movies. Would you go to a movie theatre that could monitor information about you as you watched? Why or why not?

_____

_____

③ Besides being able to identify objects, MRI can determine people's emotions. Would a phone app that identified your emotions be useful? Why or why not?

_____

_____

_____

4. It's not yet possible for software to determine most of the details you recall about a movie. Would you want an app that would help you recall details your conscious mind may have forgotten? Why or why not?

_____

_____

5. If politicians could identify your political opinions, how might this change decision-making in governments? Give one example.

_____

_____

6. The idea of being able to determine people's PIN numbers from their thoughts suggests that they will no longer be secure. What might replace PIN codes?

_____

_____

7. In a general sense, should research on improving the ability to read the brain be more carefully controlled by the government? Why or why not?

_____

_____

_____

MyBookshelf > My eLab >
Exercises > Chapter 3 >
Protecting Our Neuroprivacy

FOCUS ON SPEAKING

Making Counterarguments

When you begin a serious discussion, you are usually prepared with a set of arguments. Similarly, those with opposing points of view have their own sets of arguments. In order to go beyond just presenting, you need to examine each other's points and respond with counterarguments.

A. Counterarguments are often based on problems in the other person's logic. Imagine the topic is *online privacy* and the other speaker is arguing that it is not a concern for most people. Match the problems in logic to the example sentences.

PROBLEMS IN LOGIC		EXAMPLE SENTENCES
❶ FLAWED ANALYSIS: The speaker doesn't understand or explain the problem.	_____	a) Online privacy is a concern, but only for those who post personal information online.
❷ FLAWED FACTS: The speaker's facts are wrong or are perhaps just opinions.	_____	b) No one really cares much about privacy these days.
❸ FLAWED VALUES: The speaker is misinformed or mistaken about people's beliefs.	_____	c) If online privacy was a problem, wouldn't the government act?
❹ SUPPORTS THE OTHER SIDE'S ARGUMENT: The speaker makes points that support your ideas.	_____	d) There was no concern about online privacy a hundred years ago.
❺ TRUE BUT IRRELEVANT FACTS: The facts don't relate to the problem.	_____	e) Internet companies protect our online privacy.

Presenting a counterargument begins with recognizing and explaining problems in logic. Often, this is done with a sequence of statements:

- IDENTIFY THE PROBLEM: Online privacy requires better protection.
- SUMMARIZE WHAT THE OTHER SPEAKER SAYS: (The other speaker) suggests that online privacy is unimportant. Many people believe this is true.
- INTRODUCE EXPERT EVIDENCE: However, in a 2017 study, it was found that ...
- SUMMARIZE YOUR POINT OF VIEW: So, this all suggests that (the other speaker) is mistaken and that privacy does require better protection.

B. In Listening 1, Bob McDonald argues against all the concerns about the use of genetic data to recreate facial images. He says, "But why should I worry if somebody could see my face? I mean, people are putting their face on Facebook all the time." Use the following format to create a counterargument, then practise the discussion with a partner.

- IDENTIFY THE PROBLEM: _____

_____

- SUMMARIZE WHAT THE OTHER SPEAKER SAYS: _____

_____

- INTRODUCE EXPERT EVIDENCE: _____

_____

- SUMMARIZE YOUR POINT OF VIEW: _____

_____

In any academic discussion, it is important to always remain polite.

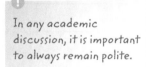

MyBookshelf > My eLab >
Exercises > Chapter 3 >
Focus on Speaking

C. With a partner, consider the following topic and adopt opposite points of view. Take turns offering counterarguments to your partner's points. Once you are confident, practise your discussion in a larger group: each student should have a chance to share and build on arguments for and against.

TOPIC: Most online privacy problems arise from people being careless.

FINAL ASSIGNMENT
Discuss Privacy in a Group

Working with a partner, use everything you have learned in this chapter to take part in a discussion on privacy. Share data from your Warm-Up Assignment (page 70) and your opinions and beliefs about that data.

A. With your partner, meet with two or more other pairs of students and introduce your topic. If possible, choose students with a different privacy topic than yours.

B. Take turns introducing your topics and summarizing the results of your Likert surveys from the Warm-Up Assignment. As the other students explain their points, use what you learned in Focus on Listening (page 56) to infer their attitudes. Share your own beliefs and opinions based on what you learned in Focus on Accuracy (page 63).

C. Use what you learned in Focus on Critical Thinking (page 57) to identify the pros and cons around the privacy issues raised by other group members. For example, licensing agreements are necessary to protect companies (pro) but can be misunderstood or overlooked by consumers (con).

D. Use what you learned in Focus on Speaking (page 75) to examine arguments and provide counterarguments. Remember to identify problems in logic in the other groups' presentations.

E. Assess your discussions and, as a group, decide how you could improve your discussion techniques next time.

Critical Connections

Listening 3 mentions the danger of an individual's genetic information revealing personal and private details about his or her family members. For example, if your cousin had a DNA test that showed a gene for a particular disease, an employer might unethically and possibly illegally learn of it and deny you job opportunities on the suspicion that you might develop the same disease.

A. Consider these three scenarios.
- Your cousin has a DNA test and, because a shared risk for a certain disease is discovered, you are able to take steps to avoid it.
- After you are fired from your job, you find out that your employer obtained access to your cousin's DNA test results and let you go out of fear of future medical costs.
- You are happily engaged to be married when your partner suddenly breaks off the relationship. You find out that her parents hired a "genetic detective" and decided, on the basis of your cousin's DNA test results, to discourage the marriage.

B. Based on the above three scenarios, what are the pros of maintaining your genetic privacy? What are the cons? Use what you learned in Focus on Accuracy (page 63) to discuss beliefs, facts, and opinions with your partner around the issues.

C. In a group, discuss the pros and cons of genetic testing and laws that might prevent genetic discrimination. Use what you learned in Focus on Accuracy to share your beliefs and opinions and what you learned in Focus on Speaking (page 75) to offer arguments and counterarguments around genetic discrimination.

CHAPTER 4

Cities for Living

Imagine you could enclose a city under a glass dome. What would happen? The city—and everyone in it— would likely soon die. On one hand, the city would be deprived of food, water, fuel, and other necessary inputs. On the other hand, waste and air pollution would accumulate. Sustainable development policies in cities aim to preserve and enhance quality of life by encouraging the wise use of resources and by minimizing pollution and other kinds of waste, often through recycling and creative building and planning solutions. How can citizens—including you—improve a city's environment and the attitudes of the people who live in it?

In this chapter, you will

- learn vocabulary related to cities and the environment;

- predict questions and answers before and while listening;

- think of hypothetical situations to predict the future;

- build cohesion and coherence with transition words;

- develop skills for taking part in panel discussions;

- learn how to interpret charts;

- identify points of view and participate in a panel discussion.

GEARING UP

A. Look at the infographic and answer the questions.

① Industry is often blamed for pollution. But why does industry remain essential for cities?

_____

② Without security, a city falls apart, but too much security can make a city unpleasant to live in. How does security technology provide a balance?

_____

_____

③ City dwellings have been changing from large family homes to apartments. Why?

_____

_____

④ Mass transit is essential for city dwellers to work, shop, and enjoy themselves. But many people prefer their cars. Why?

_____

_____

B. Compare your answers, first with a partner, then in a group. Choose the best answers.

Below are the key words you will practise in this chapter. Check the words you understand, then underline the words you use. Highlight the words you need to learn.

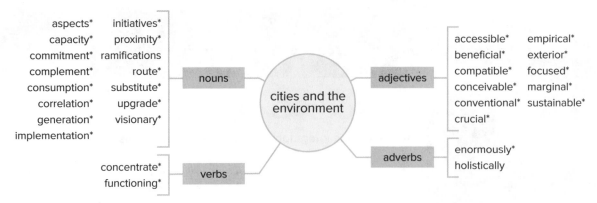

nouns

aspects*   initiatives*
capacity*   proximity*
commitment*   ramifications
complement*   route*
consumption*   substitute*
correlation*   upgrade*
generation*   visionary*
implementation*

verbs

concentrate*
functioning*

cities and the environment

adjectives

accessible*   empirical*
beneficial*   exterior*
compatible*   focused*
conceivable*   marginal*
conventional*   sustainable*
crucial*

adverbs

enormously*
holistically

*Appears on the Academic Word List

FOCUS ON LISTENING

Predicting Questions and Answers

Whether you are going to a class or for an interview, it's useful to mentally rehearse questions and answers. Anticipating a discussion helps build your listening skills by allowing you to focus on information that does and doesn't fit your predictions.

Thinking of questions and answers begins with reviewing what you know about the speaker, the topic, and the speaker's possible objectives.

A. Look at the titles of the speakers from this chapter. Predict some possible questions each might answer, based on their areas of expertise. After, compare your questions with a partner to choose the best ones, and see if you can answer them together.

SPEAKERS	QUESTION PREDICTIONS
David Byer, Vanhawks community manager	
Judith Layzer, a professor of environmental policy and planning at MIT	
Sarah Slaughter, a lecturer in sustainable business at MIT	
Milton Bevington, of the Clinton Climate Initiative	
Bill Sisson, of the Energy Efficiency in Buildings project of the World Business Council for Sustainable Development	

B. Answer the following questions, then compare answers with a partner. Choose the best ones.

1 Do you think the speakers are likely to be for or against connected bikes (even if you don't know what connected bikes are)?

_____

_____

2 Think of one or more questions you might have about connected bikes.

_____

_____

3 What do you think the speakers' objectives might be in the interviews?

_____

_____

FOCUS ON CRITICAL THINKING

Predicting the Future

You often ask yourself questions beginning with, "What if ...?" The answer is a hypothetical situation. Predicting hypothetical situations helps you explore new ideas to determine which outcomes are logical and whether those outcomes are beneficial. This is a useful critical thinking skill in academic contexts where you can consider the impacts of theoretical future changes.

A. Listening 1 talks about a world where bicycle use is changing. In this excerpt, highlight the changes that are occurring.

When it comes to cycling, habits seem to be shifting. According to *The Globe and Mail*, sales of bikes are rising. But road bike sales, the kind hard-core recreational cyclists use, are faltering. It's the sales of commuter bikes or city bikes that are picking up. Alongside that, there's been a boom in making those city bikes smart.

B. Consider the first idea in the excerpt: *cycling habits seem to be shifting*. Imagine a hypothetical situation where bicycles replaced all private cars in cities. How would that change the city? Write three predictions and then discuss them in a group. Choose the ones that would be the most and the least likely to occur.

1 *Less congestion on roads would result in more room for walking and bicycle parking and fewer fatal accidents.*

2 _____

_____

3 _____

_____

4 _____

_____

C. With a partner, consider your ideas in task B. When you think about hypothetical situations, consider possible outcomes, both positive and negative. For example, although a city without vehicles might be easier to get around and healthier, their absence for medical, fire, and police emergencies might pose a danger. In a group, consider five positive and five negative outcomes of only allowing bicycles in a city.

POSITIVE OUTCOMES	NEGATIVE OUTCOMES

LISTENING 1

Are Connected Bikes Key to Improving Urban Planning?

Since they were first invented in the late 1800s, bicycles have been an inexpensive form of transportation that has seen continuous small improvements over the years. Can bicycles now become "smart" through the use of apps?

In the following exercises, explore key words from Listening 1.

A. Identify three contexts in which each of these key words might be used.

KEY WORDS	CONTEXT 1	CONTEXT 2	CONTEXT 3
1 accessible	*parking*	*washrooms*	*wheelchairs*
2 capacity			
3 complementary			
4 exterior			
5 substitute			
6 sustainable			

B. Write a definition for each of the following key words. Work with a partner and read the definitions in random order. Ask your partner to match each definition to the correct key word. After, think of a sentence using each key word and check with your partner whether the meaning and grammar are clear.

1 capacity _____

2 focused _____

3 proximity _____

4 route _____

5 upgrade _____

C. Idioms are common in everyday communication, but they can be confusing. Match the idioms to their definitions and then, with a partner, try using each in a sentence.

IDIOMS		DEFINITIONS
1 hard-core	_____	a) solve
2 iron out	_____	b) understand and get involved with or use something creatively
3 laundry list	_____	c) sequence of processes involved in producing and delivering a product
4 supply chain	_____	d) extreme; actively committed
5 tap into	_____	e) long list of different items

Before You Listen

A. Read an excerpt from Listening 1. Besides providing directions, what other ways might a bicycle be "smart"? Discuss your ideas with a partner.

> … there's been a boom in making those city bikes smart. There are phone apps or devices you put on your bike like SmartHalo coming out this fall out of Montreal. It's a device that mounts on your handlebars and gives you turn-by-turn directions. Another more ambitious approach is to design a bike to be a smart, connected ride from the ground up.

B. Do you ride a bicycle regularly? Why or why not? If not, what is stopping you and what would make you want to ride more? Discuss your answers in a group and evaluate the best reasons for riding a bicycle.

While You Listen

C. Listen once to get the general idea. Listen again to take notes on the interviewees' responses to the host's comments and questions. Listen a third time to check your notes and add details.

HOST'S COMMENTS AND QUESTIONS	INTERVIEWEES' RESPONSES
1 We came to check out the Vanhawks Valour bike, specifically designed for the urban commuter, ...	*a carbon fibre frame keeps the weight down*
2 Some of the design features are just about making a quality bike for urban cycling.	
3 But the thing that got those Kickstarter folks so excited is the connected bike features.	• *wake the bike up:* • *it can tell*
4 LED lights in the handlebars give you turn-by-turn directions based on the route ...	*firmware and Bluetooth updates to your handlebar though your*
5 Beyond the specifics of this kind of bike, I was curious about the vision behind connected bikes. And as a cyclist in the city, I wanted to know if bikes really need a connected upgrade. So tell me about where the idea for the Valour came from.	• *idea of a bike that uses* • *goal:* • *opportunity because*
6 So we know that there are a lot of specific features of the bike, but just sort of overall, what were the kinds of shortcomings of conventional, unconnected bikes that you're trying to address?	• *shortcomings:* • *afraid to* • *sonars:* • *getting lost:* • *mission:*
7 Sohaib Zahid is the co-founder and CEO of Vanhawks. You don't get to this point without some challenges.	• *laundry list of challenges* • *supply chain and* • *bringing together*
8 Here's the thing about a connected bike, whether it's the Vanhawks Valour or just using an app on your phone ...	• *collecting* • *a million waypoints (data points on a map)*
9 So what could that potentially be used for?	• *want to build* • *tap into other routing engines:* • *want to be able to tell you about rough* • *offer*

HOST'S COMMENTS AND QUESTIONS	INTERVIEWEES' RESPONSES
⑩ So potentially, that data gathering can provide better maps, but there's more that the data can help with.	• *our plan is to be* • *it's also great for making about where to put bike lanes*
⑪ So do you imagine then that Vanhawks will be sort of like the standard or the platform ...	*software makes it better all the time and adaptable to other bikes*
⑫ So where did the idea of cyclists providing this kind of on-the-ground data for urban planners first appear?	
⑬ And so how broadly has this idea of cities creating cycling apps caught on, at least as far as you know?	• *not* • *some in Austin and San Francisco*
⑭ My hometown of Toronto has that similar app built on that same open source platform. So how effective is it compared to previous methods of gathering information about cycling habits?	• *a complement, not a* • *the cyclist population in San Francisco was around 3 to 5 percent, but they knew there were more cyclists in*
⑮ Right. I've noticed just in the last couple of weeks that on bike lanes there are a couple of those sort of, you know, cords ...	*want to know from which area to which area people are cycling*
⑯ I see. So what would urban planners, say, be using this kind of information for?	*calibrating*
⑰ I see. But is there concern that with apps like this, it's only passing on data about kind of a narrow cross-section of the population, which is to say people who have smartphones who are willing to and remember to use the app when they ride?	• *there's a bias* • *usually, it's*
⑱ Diego, we spoke to a bike manufacturer in Toronto who says that he plans to include this kind of data transmission ...	*I see a lot of potential for*
⑲ Right, Waze, which is an app that does traffic mapping but that people also supplement with their own data. But it's for cars.	*what type of data could be provided:*
⑳ I know that the MIT Senseable City Lab designed this thing called the Copenhagen Wheel ... How far do you think this kind of data collection could go in the future?	*theft concerns:*

After You Listen

D. Listening 1 mentions many cycling innovations. Are these innovations likely to make people who usually take public transportation or drive private vehicles ride a bicycle instead? Why or why not? Discuss your answers with a partner.

E. Listening 1 outlines several problems faced by cyclists that technology may help solve. Choose the best explanation for each type of problem.

❶ GLASS

    a) Weather apps can be integrated into maps to avoid the problem of glare from glass buildings on a route.

    b) Broken glass on the road will not show up on traditional digital maps but can seriously damage tires.

    c) In adverse weather conditions, the buildup of ice on roads can make them as slippery as glass.

❷ BICYCLE LANES

    a) Apps used by cyclists can help paint a picture of which bicycle lanes are most crowded so others can avoid them.

    b) When people are cycling on busy streets, apps can indicate when it is safe for them to get off the road and onto sidewalks.

    c) Fewer cars on a road can sometimes lead to too many cyclists, so an app can help space out overall usage.

❸ POLICY

    a) If most roads were replaced by bicycle lanes, it would force car owners to switch to bicycles.

    b) City officials often make decisions without enough data and randomly select where to put bicycle lanes.

    c) The sad truth is that most cities do not have the room to install bicycle lanes because of traffic congestion.

❹ THEFT

    a) Apps have become far more important than locks in stopping the increase of bicycle thefts.

    b) New technology added to bicycles may become a target for thieves.

    c) One of the major reasons people do not cycle is that bicycles are much easier to steal than cars.

❺ TRAFFIC SIGNALS

    a) Among the leading causes of bicycle accidents is that cyclists ignore traffic signals because they don't want to slow down.

    b) An intelligent app could help make bike routes faster by adjusting traffic signals to match the flow of bicycle traffic.

    c) New apps will be able to change traffic signals as cyclists approach intersections that are not too busy.

❻ ROUTES

    a) One problem with planning routes is that apps may give different directions to friends travelling the same paths through a city.

    b) The idea of planning routes often ignores real-world concerns such as going through high-crime areas of a city.

    c) The idea of customizable routes is to allow cyclists to choose paths that are not only more efficient but might also be more scenic.

7 PHONE-BASED MAPPING APPS

   a) There is a danger that cyclists will take their eyes off the road to consult their phones.

   b) Phone-based mapping apps are the most convenient way for cyclists to enjoy their trips.

   c) The current phone-based apps are more than most people need to cycle safely.

8 DATA

   a) There is no evidence that the data being collected on cycling habits reflects real-world usage.

   b) Older people tend to be the ones who can afford apps that track cycling habits.

   c) The data collected from many apps is derived more from younger cyclists who embrace technology.

MyBookshelf > My eLab >
Exercises > Chapter 4 >
Are Connected Bikes Key?

F. Despite the many advantages of bicycles, including price and portability, many people still prefer to use cars and motorcycles for transportation. Will cheaper electric cars and electric motorcycles make smart bicycles less popular? Why or why not? Discuss in a group.

FOCUS ON ACCURACY

Building Cohesion and Coherence

In conversation, it is important to follow certain rules about when and how to structure information to make it comprehensible.

A. Transition words help to show relationships between ideas. For each of the following types, add one or more examples of transition words or phrases

TRANSITION TYPES	EXAMPLES	OTHER EXAMPLES
1 cause and effect	therefore, as a result, because	
2 comparison or contrast	similarly, however, in the same way	
3 examples	for example, for instance, such as	
4 sequence	in the first place, furthermore, in addition	
5 time or location	beyond, opposite to, in the meantime	

B. A talk is cohesive if the ideas it presents stick together. It is coherent if the ideas are logical and make sense. Examine this conversation. How do the speakers relate to each other by building on one idea and adding others? Is the conversation cohesive and coherent? Why or why not?

The host uses the word challenges, *and Zahid repeats it.*

It refers to the challenge outlined in the previous sentence.

The word bridge *is a metaphor that creates the image of linking.*

> Host: You don't get to this point without some challenges.
>
> Zahid: Oh, I have a laundry list of challenges. The biggest one is supply chain and manufacturing overseas. It is a very difficult task to do when you're in North America trying to bring two industries together, cycling industry as well as electronics industry. And when two industries don't want to cooperate, you're the bridge, you're also the guy who's getting crushed in between.

One *refers to* challenges.

The phrase two industries *is repeated to connect the sentences.*

It is understood that the word between *relates to* two industries *mentioned before.*

C. Cohesive devices in the above dialogue include repetition of key words and phrases like *challenges* and *two industries*, pronouns like *one* and *it*, and conjunctions like *and, as well as,* and *also*. Read the following sentences adapted from Listening 2. Use the transition words from task A and ideas from task B to shorten and combine the sentences into one or two sentences. Practise your new sentences with a partner.

① A huge number of people live in the world's cities. Half of the world's population currently lives in cities. The number of people living in cities is steadily going up.

_____

_____

_____

② Cities remove nutrients from the landscape. Cities concentrate waste. Cities disrupt biogeochemical cycles by disturbing water flows. Cities compact soils. Cities create microclimates.

_____

_____

_____

③ Cities have a psychological effect. This psychological effect removes us from nature. We start to forget that we're really dependent on these systems functioning well. We need these systems for our own livelihoods.

_____

_____

_____

D. Although the following sentences are coherent (they make sense), they are not cohesive (they lack logical organization) because they are missing transition words. Read the sentences and then put the ideas together in a logical order. Cut out unnecessary words and add pronouns and transition words while reducing the number of sentences. Share with a partner and compare which paragraph is the most cohesive.

- Cities want to be greener.
- Greener cities are healthier.
- Reducing waste makes cities greener.
- Sustainable practices include more recycling.

MyBookshelf > My eLab >
Exercises > Chapter 4 >
Accuracy Review

_____

_____

_____

LISTENING ❷
VIDEO

Sustainability: The Next Management Frontier (Part 1)

Around the world, cities are improving their environments and making life better for their citizens. Some initiatives are top-down, such as the regulation of car use in city centres. Bottom-up initiatives include the establishment of farmers' markets and bicycle paths.

VOCABULARY BUILD

In the following exercises, explore key words from Listening 2.

A. Use five of the words in the box to complete the paragraph. Three of the words do not belong.

beneficial	commitment	compatible	crucial	empirical
functioning	initiatives	marginal		

Over the years, there have been many _____ designed to

make cities better places to live. Many of these have been aimed at the

most _____ problems of fire safety, cleanliness, and public security.

However, _____ evidence suggests that many of these changes

do not end up helping the neediest in our cities. Instead of replacing or

improving systems that are barely _____, many changes have

a _____ impact, for example, often posting regulations rather

than really enforcing them.

B. Look at the key words in bold and the three words that form collocations with each one. Write a sentence using each key word and one of the collocations. Practise your sentences with a partner, checking each other's vocabulary and grammar.

1 **beneficial:** extremely, mutually, medically

_____

2 **consumption:** excessive, conspicuous, public

_____

3 **commitment:** absolute, passionate, long-term

_____

4 **concentrate:** intently, properly, exclusively

_____

5 **compatible:** perfectly, wholly, technologically

_____

Before You Listen

A. In the video, Judith Layzer, a professor of environmental policy and planning at MIT, outlines the impacts cities have on the environment and the people who live in them.

> Cities consume three-quarters of the world's resources; they emit about 80 percent of the world's greenhouse gases. They have lots of other environmental impacts as well: they remove nutrients from the landscape, they concentrate waste, they disrupt biogeochemical cycles by disturbing water flows, compacting soils, and creating microclimates. More subtly, cities have the psychological effect of removing us from nature so we start to forget that we're really dependent on these systems functioning well for our own livelihoods.

Imagine you are a mayor or city planner. Rank the issues Layzer raises from most important (1) to least important (5).

_____ Cities consume three-quarters of the world's resources and emit about 80 percent of the world's greenhouse gases.

_____ Cities remove nutrients from the landscape.

_____ Cities concentrate waste.

_____ Cities disrupt biogeochemical cycles by disturbing water flows, compacting soils, and creating microclimates.

_____ Cities have the psychological effect of removing us from nature so we start to forget that we're really dependent on these systems functioning well for our own livelihoods.

B. What solutions can you imagine for some of the problems listed in task A? Discuss in a group as you compare your rankings.

> ❗ LEED (Leadership in Energy and Environmental Design): a set of ecology-driven building standards

While You Listen

C. Layzer shares examples from specific cities. Watch the video once to get the general idea. Watch a second time to fill in examples for each city; consider how the examples support the argument that cities will help the world become more environmentally sustainable.

CITY	EXAMPLES
❶ Boston, USA	
❷ Chicago, USA	
❸ New York, USA	
❹ Philadelphia, USA	
❺ Curitiba, Brazil	
❻ Berkeley, USA	
❼ San Francisco, USA	
❽ Portland, USA	
❾ Seattle, USA	
❿ Toronto, Canada	
⓫ Singapore, Republic of Singapore and London, England	
⓬ Qingdao, China	

CITY	EXAMPLES
13 Newark, USA	
14 Paris, France	

After You Listen

D. Consider your answers in tasks A and B above. Would you change some of your answers after listening to Layzer's arguments? Why or why not? Discuss with a partner.

E. Read the following statements and indicate whether you think each one is true or false. For each false statement, write a true one.

STATEMENTS	TRUE	FALSE
1 Boston has mandated that all new buildings meet LEED requirements or standards.		
2 The point of Chicago's permeable pavement is to help water to flow into sewers and local waterways.		
3 Philadelphia's idea of planting trees relates to future climate change.		
4 Curitiba's alternative to a park system would have been to use engineers to implement a flood control solution.		
5 Berkeley has been asking homeowners for loans to install new solar panels in the city.		
6 San Francisco's promotion of local eating means less compost will be produced.		
7 Portland's street redesign is probably meant to reduce people's dependence on cars.		

STATEMENTS	TRUE	FALSE
⑧ Singapore and London's move to charge people more to drive has reduced congestion. _____ _____		
⑨ The example of Qingdao is largely about making things more international to reduce waste. _____ _____		
⑩ Paris's free bike program encourages people to cycle on long trips. _____ _____		

MyBookshelf > My eLab >
Exercises > Chapter 4 >
Sustainability (Part 1)

F. Review the various initiatives that each city is undertaking. Which steps do you think are the most effective for improving sustainability and making cities better places to live? Compare your answers in a group and decide which measures would work best for your own or a nearby city.

WARM-UP ASSIGNMENT
Identify Two Points of View

Work with a partner. Choose a city and use what you learned in Focus on Critical Thinking (page 81) to present a hypothetical view of how that city might evolve by the year 2050.

A utopian city is a clean, comfortable environment in which people live together peacefully and have everything they need. A dystopian city is the opposite: the physical, social, and cultural environment is seriously degraded and crime is rampant. In this assignment, discuss possible future scenarios for your city.

A. Choose a city both you and your partner are familiar with and decide whether you think its future will be better or worse.
- By 2050, (name of city) will be a utopian paradise.
- By 2050, (name of city) will be a dystopian hell.

B. Research the city, keeping in mind your chosen point of view. Review the initiatives presented in Listening 2 and research other actions or strategies that could make your city a utopian paradise; alternatively, consider trends and potential problems that could make it a dystopian hell. In your research, look for statistical support for initiatives and trends indicating that situations are getting better or worse. Keep records of your sources so you can cite them when you talk. For example, to cite information from the following source,

> City of Vancouver. (2017, November). *Renewable City Action Plan*. Retrieved from http://vancouver.ca/files/cov/renewable-city-action -plan-november-2017.pdf

you could say,

> The *Renewable City Action Plan*, published by the City of Vancouver in 2017, says, ...

Visit My eLab Documents for referencing guidelines for APA, MLA, and IEEE citation styles.

C. In Listening 1 and Listening 2, you already considered how changes in cycling habits, trees, parks, building standards, control of wastewater, traffic management, and solar panels can affect quality of life. Build on these ideas and investigate inputs such as food, water, energy, and other necessities, as well as outputs such as various kinds of waste and pollution. What could happen (e.g., population increase/decrease, technology breakthroughs/breakdowns, famine/new farming innovations) that might affect the sustainability of your city?

D. When you have completed your research, summarize your points on cue cards. Discuss your points with a partner to see what details you can improve.

E. Keep your notes to refer to in the Final Assignment.

Use feedback from your teacher and classmates on this Warm-Up Assignment to improve your speaking skills.

FOCUS ON SPEAKING

Taking Part in a Panel Discussion

Whether you are interviewing someone, attending a presentation, or just making small talk, you rely on different skills to ask and direct questions. These skills are also used to express interest and elicit additional information in group and panel discussions.

Unlike group discussions, panel discussions are conducted in front of an audience that mostly listens but may ask questions.

A. In Listening 3, Sarah Slaughter, a lecturer in sustainable business at MIT, moderates a panel discussion. At various times, she leads the conversation, adds information, and directs questions or comments to individual speakers or to the group. As you read the following excerpts, consider the different ways in which Slaughter directs/moderates the discussion.

Restating or summarizing panellist comments helps lead into new questions. You remind the audience of what is important while focusing on a point or points to follow up on.

> Milton, you've been working with cities around the world.

Sometimes a statement is enough to prompt someone to speak more. If not, ask a follow-up question: "Could you tell us something about ...?"

> Well, and as you say, one of the things that's interesting is even just in the last couple of years, there's an organization which lists commercial properties and their recent analysis of the data shows that over the past two to five years, properties that have high energy performance and have reached the LEED rating for the US Green Building Council are actually selling at 10 to 15 percent premiums. And they're getting higher rents ...

> ... So one of the things that we're seeing is the market has been slow to recognize some of these values, but especially with the escalation on the energy prices, we're seeing rapid shifts in the whole market and the market economy in the trade-in quality.

Use your restatement to shift perspectives (e.g., from property owners to the whole market) and shape the conversation along specific lines.

And that leads to is a segue from one topic to another. Other expressions used in segues are: which makes me think of ...; and we can see that in ...; to follow up on ...

> And that leads to one of the other topics that we touched on briefly in our conversation yesterday, which was as we look at the new generation that's graduating from school ...

> ... And then as you were talking, Bill, in terms of managing teams, one of the things that we had touched on was the degree to which sustainability and particularly the engagement of people's hearts as well as their mind changes some of these issues. Bill, did you want to say something about that?

When several people have spoken, it's important to identify the speaker. Then, follow up with an open-ended question to that person.

It's common to direct questions to a second speaker to get a different perspective (e.g., on jobs in sustainability).

> Well, Judy, you were talking a little bit about the possibility for cities to develop new jobs as they start following industries that are sustainable and things like that. Do you want to talk about that a little bit?

B. In a small group, formulate six or more short statements on the topic of sustainability. Divide the statements among the group members.

C. Have panellists take turns presenting and explaining their statements. Students can take turns acting and use the skills outlined in task A to restate/summarize ideas, ask questions, and direct questions to the whole panel or to individuals. After, reflect on what went well and what could be improved.

MyBookshelf > My eLab > Exercises > Chapter 4 > Focus on Speaking

---

LISTENING ③
VIDEO

Sustainability: The Next Management Frontier (Part 2)

This video continues the panel discussion from Listening 2, with all four speakers: Judith Layzer, expert on environmental politics, moderator Sarah Slaughter, Milton Bevington, of the Clinton Climate Initiative, and Bill Sisson, of the Energy Efficiency in Buildings project of the World Business Council for Sustainable Development.

VOCABULARY BUILD

In the following exercises, explore key words from Listening 3.

A. Read sentences adapted from Listening 3 and choose the best meaning for each key word in bold.

1 Without the politicians, we wouldn't dream some of these dreams. I think they help make these goals **conceivable**.

    a) integral   b) unbelievable   c) possible

2 They said there is a one-to-one **correlation** between high energy costs and financial stress.

    a) difference   b) relationship   c) intervention

③ I think only to the extent that we have to think about that problem **holistically**; it is a social problem as well as an opportunity for a choice of life.

a) specifically   b) generally   c) intensely

④ For some of us that's **enormously** appealing.

a) immensely   b) generally   c) specifically

⑤ These politicians do understand how these **ramifications** play out and they can get really behind these things very quickly.

a) contraptions   b) costs   c) consequences

B. Understanding parts of words can help you quickly improve your vocabulary. Look at the bold elements of the following key words and the meaning of each element in parentheses. Write three other words that include each element. Discuss the meaning of all the words, checking your comprehension with a partner and in a dictionary.

① a**spect**s (see):

spectacle, _____

② **con**ventional (with):

_____

③ **im**plementation (in):

_____

④ **gen**eration (birth, kind):

_____

⑤ **vis**ionary (see):

_____

MyBookshelf > My eLab > Exercises > Chapter 4 > Vocabulary Review

Before You Listen

A. Read Sarah Slaughter's rather wordy opening remarks in this excerpt from the panel discussion. Rephrase the introduction to make it clearer and to make the questions more specific. Compare your version with a partner's.

So a question I have for the panel is: What is the extent to which sustainability has a competitive advantage, for a specific company, for an organization like a hospital or a university, being able to attract people, or for cities, to be able to attract people to other places?

_____

_____

_____

_____

_____

B. Based on Slaughter's question, use what you learned in Focus on Listening (page 80) to predict some questions and answers that might be asked in the panel discussion.

PREDICT QUESTIONS	PREDICT ANSWERS
1 *Is there any evidence of sustainability attracting employees?*	
2	
3	

While You Listen

C. Watch the video and take notes on each speaker's comments. Consider whether each speaker is responding to a previous speaker, asking/answering a direct question, or building on a previous topic. Watch the video again to check your notes and add details.

SPEAKER	NOTES
1 JUDITH LAYZER:	
2 SARAH SLAUGHTER:	Milton, you've been working with cities around the world.
3 MILTON BEVINGTON:	• • •
4 BILL SISSON:	
5 SARAH SLAUGHTER:	Well, and as you say, one of the things that's interesting is …
6 MILTON BEVINGTON:	
7 SARAH SLAUGHTER:	And that leads to one of the other topics that we touched on briefly in our conversation yesterday, which was …
8 BILL SISSON:	
9 SARAH SLAUGHTER:	Well, Judy, you were talking a little bit about the possibility for cities to develop new …
10 JUDITH LAYZER:	

SPEAKER	NOTES
⑪ Milton Bevington:	
⑫ Judith Layzer:	• •
⑬ Bill Sisson:	

After You Listen

D. Write a follow-up question you would like to ask one of the speakers. Practise the question with a partner and let your partner try to answer. Then, working in a group, ask and answer each other's follow-up questions. When a group member answers your question, try to think of another follow-up question to extend the discussion.

_____

_____

E. Use what you learned in Focus on Critical Thinking (page 81) to write short notes predicting what each of the following statements might imply in terms of the future. After, use what you learned in Focus on Accuracy (page 87) to put your ideas together in a short but coherent and cohesive explanation for a partner.

1 Everyone wants to live in Seattle, Portland, or Vancouver because these cities are more sustainable.

_____

2 Cities around the world compete with each other in terms of who can make the biggest promises.

_____

3 Organizations that are able to understand others, communicate, and accept new ideas are the most successful.

_____

4 Every building in California will have to be labelled in terms of its energy efficiency.

_____

5 When a building has a higher LEED certification, it can charge more in rent.

_____

6 New graduates probably want to work in newer buildings because of their status.

_____

7 The emphasis on working together is because many problems are multidisciplinary.

_____

8 The reason you can't outsource sustainability jobs is that they need to be done locally.

_____

9 Tenants can have difficulty paying rent because of increased utility costs.

_____

10 There is a continuing shift of more people moving from the suburbs to the city.

_____

_____

F. Sustainability is a concept that is being applied across a range of areas, not just to the development of cities. Use what you learned in Focus on Critical Thinking to imagine a hypothetical world in which sustainability has become a legal requirement for everyone. How would it affect your lifestyle if you had to recycle, reuse, and repurpose much more than you do now? Discuss your answers in a group and identify the changes this would require.

MyBookshelf > My eLab > Exercises > Chapter 4 > Sustainability (Part 2)

Academic
Survival Skill

Interpreting Charts

Charts help your listeners visualize lists of facts and numbers that can otherwise be difficult to imagine. But even charts can overwhelm an audience if the speaker doesn't take time to clearly point out and explain the key features.

A. Working with a partner, review the following graphic from Montreal, Canada. Choose three elements that you understand and explain them to a partner, adding examples. Circle the segments of the graphic you find difficult to understand.

B. Look at the following chart, which compares the amounts of various types of waste that are recycled. On a separate page, write three statements related to different elements in the chart and explain what could be done to improve recycling and make cities more sustainable. Consider using comparative and superlative statements such as, "Six times more plastic than metal is recycled" and "People recycle plastic the most and metal the least."

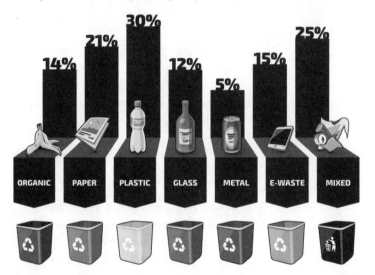

C. Discuss the chart in a group, sharing your observations. Try to add reasons why you think some waste is recycled more than others. For example, which of the above are you most likely to recycle? Why?

FINAL ASSIGNMENT

Participate in a Panel Discussion

Now it's your turn. Use everything you have learned in this chapter to prepare for and participate in a panel discussion on a hypothetical situation, as explored in Focus on Critical Thinking (page 81).

A. Form groups of six and use what you learned in Focus on Speaking (page 94) to discuss this question:

• Will future cities be more utopian or dystopian? Why?

B. Select a moderator for your group. The moderator's job is to introduce the topic and the panel members, as well as to elicit, rephrase, and direct audience questions to the right panel member. The moderator can also present.

C. Meet as a group to identify roles reflecting different points of view on the topic, based on what you discussed in the Warm-Up Assignment (page 93). Choose your role based on one of the following occupations or think of another.

☐ architect   ☐ pollution specialist

☐ business professional   ☐ recycling expert

☐ crime specialist   ☐ solar panel expert

☐ farmer   ☐ transportation expert

☐ natural disaster expert   ☐ urban planner

☐ politician   ☐ other role: _____

D. Find a chart, graph, infographic, or photograph on the Internet that helps to illustrate your point of view. Use what you learned in Academic Survival Skill (page 99) to think of how you will share and explain the image to the panel and audience. Use what you learned in Focus on Listening (page 80) to anticipate questions and answers.

E. Practise your panel discussion with your moderator, each playing your own role. Use what you learned in Focus on Listening to anticipate questions and answers, and what you learned in Focus on Accuracy (page 87) to add ideas to make the conversation coherent and cohesive.

F. Present your panel discussion in front of the class. After, meet to reflect on what went well and what could have gone better.

Critical Connections

A key concern of any city is the flow of goods, services, and people. But some people have greater challenges navigating the city.

A. Consider the following quotation.

> We are all physically disabled at some time in our lives. A child, a person with a broken leg, a parent with a pram, an elderly person, etc., are all disabled in one way or another ... As far as the built-up environment is concerned, it is important that it should be barrier-free and adapted to fulfill the needs of all people equally. As a matter of fact, the needs of the disabled coincide with the needs of the majority, and all people are at ease with them. (United Nations, 2003–04)
>
> United Nations. (2004). *Accessibility for the disabled: A design manual for a barrier free environment.* Retrieved from https://static.un.org/esa/socdev/enable/designm/index.html

B. In a group, brainstorm the barriers that people face in moving around within cities. These barriers can be physical, as suggested in the quote, or psychological; for example, issues such as garbage on the streets can make some parts of a city less appealing.

C. Use what you've learned in this chapter and imagine that you and your group members are all part of a panel discussion. Consider the hypothetical situation of a city that would be more accessible to everyone, regardless of any disabilities. If we could create such a city, what would it look like?

CHAPTER 5

The Creative Solution

As a thinking machine, you are exceptionally good at solving problems. Solving problems sometimes involves thinking about how you achieved past successes, such as a particular way you studied for a test. Other times, you remember what others have done to solve similar problems. But in many cases, the problem is new and you need to use your brain to think of a creative solution. Research on creativity and problem-solving are ongoing, exploring how and why some brains function differently and how machines might be taught to think as humans do. What do you understand about your brain and ways to improve your creativity, memory, and thought processes?

In this chapter, you will

- learn vocabulary related to creativity and problem-solving;

- listen for logical fallacies;

- explore problems and solutions;

- explain abstract ideas through examples;

- learn to identify problems and evaluate arguments;

- present reasons, causes, and explanations using connectors;

- describe a problem and take part in a creative consultation.

GEARING UP

A. Look at the diagram and answer the questions.

From Idea to Process

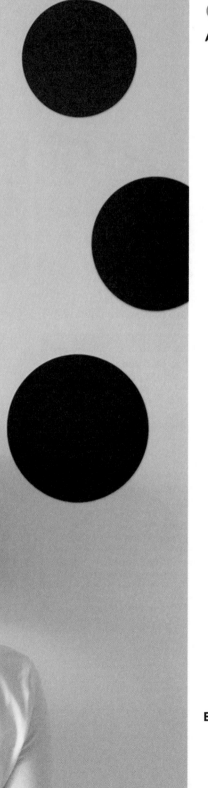

PROCESS
CONCEPT
CREATIVE
VISION
IDEA

1 We make use of creative ideas to solve old problems in new ways, starting with a *vision* based on objectives. Besides completing your courses and graduating, what are your other objectives for studying at university?

_____

2 A *concept* can refer to a new idea or plan to solve a problem. Studying in university requires acquiring a lot of new vocabulary. What new and different concept can you think of for studying and remembering vocabulary?

_____

_____

3 The creative *process* often involves trying things out and learning from mistakes. Does university support the idea of trial and error (learning from your mistakes)? Why or why not?

_____

_____

4 Being creative involves looking for innovative conclusions and solutions beyond the usual, obvious ones. What new methods might replace university learning in the future?

_____

_____

B. Compare your answers, first with a partner, then in a group. Choose the best answers.

Below are the key words you will practise in this chapter. Check the words you understand, then underline the words you use. Highlight the words you need to learn.

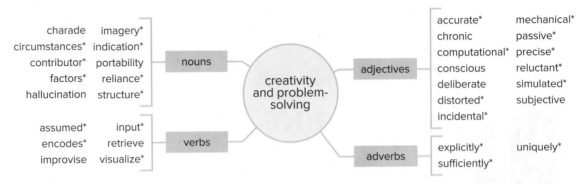

nouns

charade imagery*
circumstances* indication*
contributor* portability
factors* reliance*
hallucination structure*

verbs

assumed* input*
encodes* retrieve
improvise visualize*

creativity and problem-solving

adjectives

accurate* mechanical*
chronic passive*
computational* precise*
conscious reluctant*
deliberate simulated*
distorted* subjective
incidental*

adverbs

explicitly* uniquely*
sufficiently*

*Appears on the Academic Word List

FOCUS ON LISTENING

Listening for Logical Fallacies

In an ideal world, people would openly share and discuss ideas and be ready to accept better ones. But often, people view discussions as battles they must win, whether or not their ideas are the best ones. When you listen, you need to learn to recognize logical fallacies (flaws in reasoning) in speakers' arguments that lead to false conclusions.

A. Work with a partner to match the logical fallacies to the correct definitions.

LOGICAL FALLACIES		DEFINITIONS
1 APPEAL TO EMOTION	_____	a) presenting two disagreeable choices when other choices might be available
2 APPEAL TO IGNORANCE	_____	b) suggesting that doing one thing is certain to lead to a terrible result (when it may not)
3 FALSE DILEMMA	_____	c) saying two things are the same when they are not really alike
4 FAULTY ANALOGY	_____	d) using strong feelings instead of facts to encourage some action
5 SLIPPERY SLOPE	_____	e) starting a debate with a false idea that doesn't support the argument
6 FALSE PREMISES	_____	f) saying that nobody knows the answer, so one particular idea must be true

B. Read the sentences related to ideas from Listening 1. Work with a partner and write the logical fallacy each one illustrates. Explain why they are logical fallacies.

1 Your mind is like a locked room with a filing cabinet in it.

_____

_____

_____

2 You can either have a phone and keep in contact with people or you can lose all your friends.

_____

_____

3 Of course everyone wants a phone, but then they want a second phone, and soon people will be carrying around three or more phones.

_____

_____

4 It's impossible to know how much people depend on their phones to store ideas, so they must do so a lot.

_____

_____

5 Can you imagine having a bunch of accidents like Patrick Jones and losing your memory? If you truly feel sorry for him, you should donate $100.

_____

_____

C. Listening 1 talks about the phone as an extension of the mind. Yet students are often discouraged from using their phones in class because they are distractions. In a group, think of five logical fallacies that are, or could be, used to criticize phone usage. As each student suggests a logical fallacy, try to identify what kind it is. Then, together, think of one solution to the problem of phones in the classroom that doesn't involve taking them away.

_____

_____

FOCUS ON CRITICAL THINKING

Exploring Problems and Solutions

You solve countless problems every day. Problems can be as simple as finding time to study or as complex as having to decide what degree and career to pursue. In discussions with others, it is important to be able to clearly identify the problem in order to consider appropriate solutions.

A. When you listen, it is necessary to recognize expressions people might use to refer to problems and solutions. Think of three other words or expressions you could use in place of the words in bold. After, share your answers in a group to see how many different ways there are to talk about problems and solutions.

1 I have **a problem with** remembering things.

_____   _____   _____

2 One **solution** might be to write lists.

_____   _____   _____

B. The table below lists six common problem-solving techniques. With a partner, read the example problem beside each one, then suggest another one for which the technique would be useful.

TECHNIQUES	EXAMPLE PROBLEMS
❶ TRIAL AND ERROR (trying different approaches until one works)	• a physics experiment designed to see how much weight a bridge can carry
❷ ALGORITHMS (following already familiar procedures)	• using a formula with several steps to search for materials online
❸ DEDUCTIVE REASONING (starting with a conclusion and seeing if data supports it)	• wondering if you can predict the content of a lecture from its title
❹ INDUCTIVE REASONING (making broad generalizations from examples)	• noticing a teacher gives tests on the same day each week and assuming he or she will probably do so again
❺ HEURISTICS (using rules of thumb that have worked in the past)	• learning that something takes two to three hours of study for every hour in class
❻ DIALECTICAL REASONING (comparing pros and cons)	• deciding between buying two computers

C. The first step in solving a problem is to make sure you understand the issues that led up to it; it might be necessary to redefine the problem to highlight the most important issue. Read the following excerpt from Listening 1 and explain what the problem is. Then, in a group, discuss how you might solve the problem.

> (Patrick Jones has) become somebody who can't lay down new memories. So, if you had a chat with Patrick Jones and then you left the room, and then you came back in ten minutes later … he wouldn't be able to remember who you were or what you chatted about.

_____

_____

_____

_____

_____

Your Phone Is an Extension of Your Mind

What tools and technologies do you rely on to help you think and solve life's problems? You may still use traditional tools like paper diaries and lists, but you have also probably come to rely on your phone for information and inspiration. How much should you depend on technology to help you remember and solve problems? Also, if people's phones are an extension of their minds, what laws or restrictions should be placed on governments about searching them?

VOCABULARY BUILD	In the following exercises, explore key words from Listening 1.

A. Working with a partner, think of a solution to each of the problems. Use the key words in bold in your replies.

❶ Most people have **distorted** views of the past, often idealizing what life was like when they were younger.

_____

_____

❷ By increasing the **portability** of everyday things like folding chairs, there is often a loss of comfort.

_____

_____

❸ Most people learn complex ideas online but find it difficult to **retrieve** and apply them when they are needed.

_____

_____

❹ People—especially teenagers and seniors—are often frustrated at bank machines because it is easy to **input** the wrong numbers.

_____

_____

B. Choose the best word from each pair to fill in the blanks in the sentences that follow. Compare your answers with a partner. How do the meanings of the two words differ?

❶ explicitly / sufficiently

a) Although your phone can store many things you don't need to remember,

you shouldn't always have to _____ think that you have to look at your phone to find information.

b) So I think that the smartphone by now has become _____ interwoven with people's normal activities that we can assume owning one will always be the norm.

2 incidental / passive

    a) Your _____ memory includes the sorts of things that you don't need to use from day to day.

    b) Although many people doodle (draw or scribble) when they talk,

      it's probably _____ to how they remember ideas.

3 deliberate / conscious

    a) I don't actually, as a _____ agent, know what those roles are.

    b) The more you have to bottleneck it through those sorts of _____ thoughts, the less it looks like part of the machinery of the mind.

4 precise / chronic

    a) A _____ problem that some people have is always forgetting things like others' names.

    b) The "aha" moment is just one very _____ operation in the brain that doesn't always happen.

C. The following are uncommon words and phrases used in Listening 1. Match each one to its meaning.

WORDS AND PHRASES		MEANINGS
1 Evernote trails	*c*	a) bodies improved by the integration of digital or mechanical devices
2 doodling	_____	b) the scope of what you can learn
3 cyborgs	_____	c) sequential notes on a topic
4 cognitive horizon	_____	d) tendency to do well at something
5 proclivity	_____	e) the memory in your head
6 bio-memory	_____	f) scribbling or sketching absent-mindedly

Before You Listen

A. Read an excerpt from Listening 1 that raises questions about what goes on in your brain when you think. After, think about a simple task such as putting on a hat. What thoughts is it necessary to connect to accomplish this?

Do you ever think about thinking? I mean, what's really going on in our minds when we think? Maybe your mind is like a locked room with a filing cabinet in it. When you remember to buy the milk on your way home, it's like your mind picked the right file out of the cabinet. Or maybe your mind is like a computer. You input information and the right answer pops out. Either way, it feels like something is going in here, inside my brain, which takes inputs from the outside world and somehow turns it into what the mind comes up with. Memories, feelings, ideas ... Only what if that's not the right way to think about minds at all?

_____

_____

_____

_____

B. The title of Listening 1 is "Your Phone Is an Extension of Your Mind." In what ways does your phone extend your mind and thinking processes? Discuss your answers in a group, then rank your combined ideas in order of importance.

While You Listen

C. In Focus on Listening (page 104) and Focus on Critical Thinking (page 105), you explored aspects of problems and solutions. As you listen, read the problems and points and fill in solutions and ideas that expand on them. After, discuss your notes with a partner and try to come up with better solutions.

PROBLEMS AND POINTS	SOLUTIONS AND IDEAS
❶ PROBLEM: Does the mind work on its own?	_Andy Clark argues for extended minds, meaning the mind includes things around you in your environment that you use to help you think._
❷ PROBLEM: not knowing your friend's phone number or needing the answer to a question	
❸ PROBLEM: bio-memory is unreliable	
❹ PROBLEM: features a technology or an external tool needs to have to be considered, you know, to make the cut as it were for extended minds?	
❺ POINT: accessing an encyclopedia in the basement	
❻ PROBLEM: other mental functions like creative thought	
❼ PROBLEM: getting to an "aha" moment	
❽ POINT: Is doodling (scribbling or sketching absent-mindedly) a waste of time?	
❾ POINT: Why develop language?	
❿ POINT: how we differ from animals	
⓫ POINT: The idea of extended minds is kind of a troubling notion.	

PROBLEMS AND POINTS	SOLUTIONS AND IDEAS
12 POINT: the whole raft of ethical issues	
13 POINT: Is a phone part of your anatomy?	
14 PROBLEM: Patrick Jones can't lay down new memories.	
15 PROBLEM: people who twenty years ago would have been in 24/7 care	

After You Listen

D. The problems in While You Listen are not all described using full sentences. With a partner, take turns stating both the problems and solutions as full sentences. As you do so, check your notes to ensure that you both agree and that you have identified the best solutions to the problems.

E. Choose the best answer to complete each sentence.

1 Smartphones are now considered a bit of the machinery of our minds because _____.

   a) people, especially teenagers, have difficulty not thinking about them

   b) they have become interwoven with our normal abilities and activities

   c) they are modelled on the ways that we listen, speak, and think

2 The example of thinking about which month it is explains _____.

   a) how bio-memory is more automatic than looking at a phone

   b) why phones that keep track of the month are superior to memory

   c) that there are easy functions on a phone that are completely unnecessary

3 An example of how information falls into patterns that make sense with other patterns might be _____.

   a) looking at your phone and wondering if you have missed any calls or texts

   b) seeing a new plant and considering how it compares to other plants you know

   c) studying one subject at university and then switching to another new subject

4 The habit of making little marks in the margin of books _____.

   a) is mentioned to point out how memories can be damaged by others

   b) is an example of how people influence others by adding to printed content

   c) likely has a cognitive purpose although the purpose is unclear

5 An example of how language can be considered an extended mind technology is _____.

   a) relying on written materials instead of having to remember everything

   b) talking to ourselves to remember what we have to do

   c) the way we sometimes remember an idea only after someone mentions it to us

6 The idea that we get a distorted picture of what mind and cognition are has to do with _____.

   a) how often we look and think about things that we should already know about

   b) thinking about what we learn in school and university and what we learn in life

   c) not seeing them as part of a complex ecology that includes the body and the surrounding world

7 An early sense that we could all become cyborgs might come from devices such as _____.

   a) Global Positioning System (GPS) satellites that provide location information

   b) televisions and radios that bring us news we don't have time to read about

   c) wearable hearing aids that amplify sounds but also connect to our phones

8 The idea of your phone and other digital devices being related to your anatomy _____.

   a) is unrelated to the costs involved except when you have to replace a device

   b) raises concerns around privacy, as they are extensions of your body and mind

   c) means that you can wear them on your body like pieces of clothing

9 The Evernote trails Patrick Jones makes as he moves through the world are _____.

   a) things most of us naturally remember about other people and events

   b) meant to guide others who will eventually follow his same pathways

   c) invisible except to someone who forgets about digital devices

10 Interfering with bio-external support for someone like Patrick Jones would be serious because _____.

   a) the Supreme Court has set prison sentences for doing so

   b) he depends on it for his daily interactions with other people

   c) no one knows what would happen if he was deprived of it

F. Although technology like phones can be extensions of your mind, they also often distract you from your work. Gamble (2016) says, "Every great work of culture, be it a scientific breakthrough or a literary masterpiece, was achieved by a person who, at minimum, was able to pay attention" (p. 64). With a partner, discuss whether technology distracts you from being creative. Why or why not?

MyBookshelf > My eLab > Exercises > Chapter 5 > Your Phone Is an Extension of Your Mind

Reference

Gamble, J. (2016). Caught in the net. *New Philosopher, 11*, 64–65.

FOCUS ON SPEAKING

Explaining Abstract Ideas through Examples

When you talk about abstract ideas and solutions to problems, examples help to illustrate your points in concrete ways. Rather than asking an audience to simply imagine how a theoretical idea might work, you can offer examples that illustrate how the hypothetical situation might be applied in real life.

You can use five common words and phrases to introduce examples:

• FOR EXAMPLE: the most common form

• FOR INSTANCE: slightly less formal than *for example*

• SUCH AS: usually used mid-sentence

• LIKE: used in the same way as *such as*

• NAMELY: unlike the above, *namely* lists all the parts of a group, not just one or two of them

A. Read the sentences and choose the word or phrase in parentheses that best completes each one according to the above explanations.

   1 We tend to think of memory in terms of two extremes, (namely / for example) remembering and forgetting.

   2 There are many diseases related to memory loss, (like / namely) Alzheimer's.

   3 (For instance / Like), some people use tools to help them remember.

   4 (Such as / For example), my aunt started losing her memory at age fifty.

   5 Four main parts of the brain are involved with memory, (namely / such as) the amygdala, the hippocampus, the cerebellum, and the prefrontal cortex.

   6 Some people claim that certain foods (such as / namely) avocados help your memory.

B. Work with a partner and complete the answers to the questions based on Listenings 1, 2, and 3.

  ① Clark talks about where the mind stops and the rest of the world begins, suggesting that technology helps support our thinking. What are one or two examples?

    For example, _____

    _____

  ② People often talk about the "aha" moment when you suddenly see the solution to the problem. Can you share an instance of an "aha" moment you've had?

    Yes, **for instance,** _____

    _____.

  ③ We're headed into a future where we will have lots more technology and more technology that's really embedded in our lives.

    It's true. We will all eventually have embedded technology **such as**

    _____

    _____

  ④ So, we're just talking about ordinary people who are not professional journalists who want to get involved with telling stories in their communities. What sorts of communities do people belong to?

    People tend to belong to many communities, **like** _____

    _____

  ⑤ There are systems that can paint pictures or systems that can do visual things, **such as** putting the right colours together in a picture. What are a couple of other unusual things that computers are doing these days?

    There are things **such as** _____

    _____.

  ⑥ Attitudes toward computers are basically broken into two opinions,

    namely _____

MyBookshelf > My eLab > Exercises > Chapter 5 > Focus on Speaking

LISTENING ❷   Aphantasia: When the Mental Image Is Missing

Try to picture yourself standing on an ice shelf in Antarctica surrounded by thousands of penguins. Even though you may never have been to Antarctica or seen a penguin, if you're like most people, you can imagine the scenario. But a small percentage of people have a condition known as *aphantasia*, meaning they cannot visualize objects or abstract concepts in their minds. They understand information and recognize scenes in front of them, but they cannot create mental images.

A. Read sentences from Listening 2 and choose the best meaning for each key word in bold.

1. It's sort of been below the radar because people who do imagine things have always **assumed** that everyone was just like them.

    a) supported

    b) suppressed

    c) supposed

2. Dr. Adam Zeman, a neurologist at the University of Exeter in the UK, published a case study about a man who had lost the ability to **visualize** things after he had angioplasty.

    a) imagine

    b) impart

    c) impress

3. I think it would be more **accurate** to say that he didn't know that other people didn't have it.

    a) consistent

    b) contradictory

    c) correct

4. Everybody around me in the world has been carrying on this massive **charade** to try and pretend as though the world is something different from the way it is.

    a) preoperative

    b) pretence

    c) preoccupation

5. We've made a decision and we're aware of that decision, whereas it's the nature of a **hallucination** that you have the sense that you're perceiving something which is out there in the world and which you haven't chosen to visualize.

    a) deterioration

    b) delusion

    c) distrust

B. Working with a partner, read the following sentences and replace each key word with a synonym. Write the synonym in the space following the key word. Look up those key words you do not know. Check to make sure you have not changed any meanings.

1. Freelance **contributor** _____ Alison Motluk joins me now to discuss this neurological quirk and what might be behind it.

2. It's this weird condition of not being able to create mental **imagery**

    _____.

3. The big tower in Toronto? Yeah, it was the tallest free-standing **structure**

    _____ when it was built.

4 I mean, he also said that people were very **reluctant** _____ to believe him when he first told them.

5 Michelle says she **encodes** _____ everything in terms of words.

C. Idioms are expressions that are not always easy to understand from the individual words that form them. Their meanings must be learned. Read four idioms from Listening 2, write what they mean, then, with a partner, try using each one in a sentence.

1 things in our heads: _____

2 pulling peoples' legs: _____

3 hard time: _____

4 mind's eye: _____

Before You Listen

A. Read an excerpt from Listening 2 and answer the questions. Look up any words you don't know.

> A few years ago, Dr. Adam Zeman, a neurologist at the University of Exeter in the UK, published a case study about a man who had lost the ability to visualize things after he had angioplasty. And since that's kind of a cool story, the American science writer Carl Zimmer wrote about it, about how this poor fellow lost an ability that all of us have. Well, twenty-one people wrote to Dr. Zeman after that saying, "Uh, don't know what you're talking about. I've never been able to visualize things."

1 A neurologist is someone who _____.

a) is concerned with memory loss

b) studies brain-damaged patients

c) operates on damaged nerves

2 An angioplasty is _____.

a) a procedure to unblock blood vessels

b) an operation on the upper part of the brain

c) a mental condition related to uncontrolled anger

3 The fact that twenty-one people wrote to Zeman suggests that _____.

a) he is a popular writer and his article caused public interest

b) only a small portion of readers were interested in him

c) the condition was not as isolated as he thought

B. People who have aphantasia have difficulty explaining their condition to others. Suppose you are talking to someone about how you picture things in your mind. How would you explain it? Write your answer, then try explaining it to a partner.

_____

_____

_____

While You Listen

C. Listen carefully to the ideas and complete the notes on the key points.

KEY POINTS	NOTES
❶ something people with aphantasia cannot imagine	*a pasture with a white horse grazing in the shade of a willow tree right next to a babbling brook*
❷ how a person with aphantasia imagines the CN Tower	*it's _____ , it's _____ , it has that bulging disk up* _____
❸ Dr. Zeman published results, which led to quite a bit more media coverage, and thousands of people came forward	*one of them was*
❹ he didn't know that other people didn't have it	*he didn't know that other people*
❺ here's how John describes the discovery	• *profoundly* • *it was like everyone had been carrying on a massive* • *or that maybe he'd* • *it was like learning*
❻ when you tell somebody about aphantasia for the first time	*stages of reactions:* • *think it's totally* • *express* • *shocked* • *think you're* • *insist you're* • *get irate (angry)* • *consider visual images as*
❼ visual imagery in your mind	*you choose*
❽ a hallucination	*you haven't*
❾ he has an amazing memory	• *has learned five hundred* • *expert* • *has a huge vocabulary in* • *is a*
❿ John remembers things as facts	*numbers or* *proportions* *its texture, or its*
⓫ he reads a lot	*his home is literally*

KEY POINTS	NOTES
⑫ John doesn't develop a visual image of what's going on when he's reading	*he just understands the plot as*
⑬ John doesn't understand the long descriptive passages in novels	*for example, novels written*
⑭ she's an author creating worlds in her mind, but she can't even see them	*Michelle says she*
⑮ Michelle's accomplishment is similar to the experience of	*someone who can't see*
⑯ she doesn't conjure images, but she does conjure some things,	*like the*
⑰ the patient performed rather well on standard tests of visual imagery	*he would be able to tell us which was darker,*
⑱ brain-imaging experiment: he had entirely normal brain activation just as you or I would	*if we were*

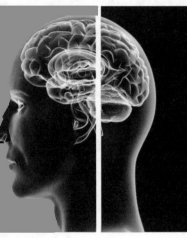

After You Listen

D. Based on what you now understand about aphantasia, write a short definition in one or two sentences. Compare definitions with a partner, then, together, write a better one based on your shared ideas.

_____

_____

E. Write a response to each of the following questions. After, discuss your answers with a partner and choose the best ones.

① Why is it significant that people with aphantasia are able to describe things they cannot see in their minds?

_____

_____

② Why had people with aphantasia not come forward before Carl Zimmer wrote about Dr. Zeman's case study?

_____

_____

③ Why might people with aphantasia be disturbed when they first find out about their condition?

_____

_____

④ Why might those with aphantasia prefer non-fiction to fiction literature?

_____

_____

⑤ Why is it surprising that Michelle Sagara has aphantasia?

_____

_____

⑥ What examples point to aphantasia as a spectrum condition that affects people in different ways and to varying degrees?

_____

_____

⑦ What point is made about aphantasia and the ability to visualize faces?

_____

_____

F. Working in a group, look at the picture on the right for one minute, then put it away. On a separate page, write a description of what you remember seeing. Share your descriptions with the group, then look at the picture again and consider any details you may have added or forgotten. What surprises you? Do you think people with aphantasia would be more or less likely to accurately describe what they remembered if they did this task?

MyBookshelf > My eLab >
Exercises > Chapter 5 >
Aphantasia

Academic
Survival Skill

Identifying Problems and Evaluating Arguments

You often encounter problems that require creative solutions—or new ways of addressing situations. The same is true for businesses. However, it can often be challenging to pinpoint the exact problem and evaluate arguments in favour of a particular solution.

A. Many people argue that creative computers might become increasingly common in the arts and will be able to produce songs, paintings, novels, and video scripts. Read the following steps and example problems and arguments. In the fifth step, explain whether you agree or disagree with the arguments.

STEPS	EXAMPLE PROBLEMS AND ARGUMENTS
1 Understand the topic and the point that is being argued. For example, what is the problem and what is the proposed solution? A solution is sometimes referred to as a *conclusion*.	"Professional musicians are expensive but soon, intelligent robots will be able to replace them." The problem is the *expense* and the solution is using *robots* instead of people.
2 Identify the *stated premises*—the facts or opinions that the speaker uses to support the conclusion.	The stated premise is that "musicians are expensive".
3 Identify the *unstated premises*—assumptions that speakers and listeners may take for granted, but which may be false.	The unstated premise is that people don't care whether they are listening to music made by a real person or a robot.
4 Challenge the premises, arguing whether or not they apply to the problem and solution.	• Although professional musicians may be highly paid, their wages are a reflection of society's values. • People may not want to listen to music by robots.
5 Decide if the premises support the conclusion or naturally lead to the solution.	

B. Listening 1 focused on memory. Read the following five recommendations (solutions) on how to help yourself remember things. Which do you think would be the most and the least effective, and why? Number the recommendations from 1 (most effective) to 5 (least effective). Discuss your answers with a partner.

_____ Get a tutor to keep up with challenging courses.

_____ Write detailed lists of what you want to say before every meeting you attend.

_____ Write to-do lists and keep them handy so you can refer to them often.

_____ Place sticky note reminders in places where you won't miss them.

_____ Write the steps in any new procedure you learn, no matter how simple.

C. With a partner, choose one of the above memory solutions and evaluate it in terms of the steps in task A. Note: in some cases, there may not be any stated premises.

STEPS FOR RECOMMENDATION # _____	PROBLEMS AND ARGUMENTS
1 Understand the topic and the point that is being argued.	
2 Identify the stated premises.	
3 Identify the unstated premises.	
4 Challenge the premises, arguing whether or not they apply to the problem and solution.	
5 Decide if the premises support the conclusion or naturally lead to the solution.	

WARM-UP ASSIGNMENT
Describe a Problem to Find a Creative Solution

Listening 1 focused on how technology extends your mind and Listening 2, on a problem some people have in visualizing things or concepts. Many problems could benefit from creative solutions, particularly ones that use technology.

A. Consider these brain-related problems and, with a partner, choose one that interests you.

- ANXIETY DISORDER: frequently experiencing unjustified fear and worry
- COLOUR BLINDNESS: inability to differentiate between colours, such as red and green
- DYSLEXIA: difficulties with accurate and/or fluent word recognition and poor spelling and decoding abilities
- INSOMNIA: inability to sleep
- MATHEMATICS DISORDER SYMPTOM: difficulty in working with numbers
- MEMORY LOSS: difficulty remembering things
- TINNITUS: sensation of ringing in the ears

Visit My eLab Documents for referencing guidelines for APA, MLA, and IEEE citation styles.

B. Research the problem to learn more about it. Keep a record of your sources. Write a statement defining the problem and explaining why it is significant. For example, you might argue that a certain condition interferes with students completing their studies.

_____

C. Exchange statements with another pair of students. Each pair then plays devil's advocate and challenges the other pair's ideas using the steps learned in Academic Survival Skill (page 118). Also use what you learned in Focus on Listening (page 104) to identify any logical fallacies. Fill in the table with feedback from other students on your problem and arguments.

STEPS	PROBLEM AND ARGUMENTS
❶ Understand the topic and the point that is being argued.	
❷ Identify the stated premises.	
❸ Identify the unstated premises.	
❹ Challenge the premises, arguing whether or not they apply to the problem and solution.	
❺ Decide if the premises support the conclusion or naturally lead to the solution.	

Use feedback from your teacher and classmates on this Warm-Up Assignment to improve your speaking skills.

D. Based on your ideas about the problem, brainstorm a solution involving technology. For example, would an existing or new app help? Use what you learned in Focus on Speaking (page 112) to provide examples. Ensure that you have no logical fallacies. Take notes on what you can improve when you share your ideas and answer questions in the Final Assignment.

Can a Computer Be Creative?

Creativity is a necessary part of problem-solving. Creative people tend to disregard rules in favour of new and interesting approaches. Often, this leads to unexpected and surprising results, such as the innovative ways the artist Picasso came up with to depict the human form. But can creative ideas be broken down into rules that computers can learn and subsequently learn to break? Can computers teach you more about problem-solving?

VOCABULARY BUILD

In the following exercises, explore key words from Listening 3.

A. Identify three contexts in which each key word might be used.

KEY WORDS	CONTEXT 1	CONTEXT 2	CONTEXT 3
❶ circumstances	*a person's unfortunate childhood*		
❷ improvise		*fixing a broken appliance*	
❸ indication			*a medical condition*
❹ mechanical		*automatic responses to questions*	
❺ simulated	*an imaginary reality, such as in video games*		

B. For each of the following key words, identify the root word. Also, indicate the part of speech of each key word and root word. With a partner, try using each key word and its root word in a sentence.

KEY WORDS	PARTS OF SPEECH	ROOT WORDS	PARTS OF SPEECH
❶ computational	*adjective*	*compute*	*verb*
❷ factors			
❸ reliance			
❹ subjective			
❺ uniquely			

MyBookshelf > My eLab > Exercises > Chapter 5 > Vocabulary Review

Before You Listen

A. Read an excerpt from Listening 3 and answer the questions.

> What we don't accept is the idea that computers could add something in that they're not being programmed to do. They could do something creative. If a computer is just a machine, how can it do these creative things? How can it be inspired? How can it work with new ideas? We think of creativity as something that's uniquely human, something that needs more than mechanical processing, but recently, one area of artificial intelligence has looked at exactly this question. Can computers also be creative?

Pablo Picasso

1 Computers and other digital devices often do unexpected things. Why do we consider these things as problems and not a sign of creativity?

_____

_____

_____

2 Why do we think of creativity as something that's uniquely human?

_____

_____

_____

3 Is creativity a sign of intelligence, artificial or otherwise? Why or why not?

_____

_____

_____

B. What are some possible dangers of computers and other digital devices being creative in terms of solving everyday problems? For example, would you want your car, microwave, or fridge to be creative? What sorts of choices might they make? In a group, discuss the worst-case scenario if people's smart home appliances suddenly decided to act on their own.

While You Listen

C. Listen once and list the stated premise for each argument, using what you learned in Academic Survival Skill (page 118). Listen a second time to consider and write down any unstated premises. After, compare your notes with a partner to add premises you may have missed.

ARGUMENTS	PREMISES
1 … we have been more accustomed to the idea of computers being able to do more intelligent things …	STATED PREMISE: _we think computers are being more intelligent_ UNSTATED PREMISE: _we consider intelligence in terms of the things computers can do_
2 computer software can do all sorts of creative things: write plots for musicals and songs …	STATED PREMISE: UNSTATED PREMISE:
3 They do this in different ways. Different systems work in different ways.	STATED PREMISE: UNSTATED PREMISE:
4 And that's one of the major reasons why we do computational creativity.	STATED PREMISE: UNSTATED PREMISE:

ARGUMENTS	PREMISES
5 And actually, it's a really difficult question.	STATED PREMISE: UNSTATED PREMISE:
6 Creativity is a different thing in different circumstances …	STATED PREMISE: UNSTATED PREMISE:
7 So one thing that we do in computational creativity is to work out what it actually means to be creative.	STATED PREMISE: UNSTATED PREMISE:
8 I found that the words represented fourteen different areas which are part of creativity, …	STATED PREMISE: UNSTATED PREMISE:
9 Some of these factors become more important than others …	STATED PREMISE: UNSTATED PREMISE:
10 If you're dealing with a system that can improvise music, quite often when people improvise music, …	STATED PREMISE: UNSTATED PREMISE:
11 … three factors came out as the most important ….	STATED PREMISE: good improvisation is based on three things: UNSTATED PREMISE:
12 I wrote a system which is able to improvise music …	STATED PREMISE: UNSTATED PREMISE:
13 My system was the little grey line that's at the bottom there, not doing so well …	STATED PREMISE: UNSTATED PREMISE:
14 And somehow, I have this fascinating challenge ahead of me, …	STATED PREMISE: UNSTATED PREMISE:
15 And in the same way, it's quite helpful to think of computers in this way. They're the small child learning to develop their creativity …	STATED PREMISE: UNSTATED PREMISE:

After You Listen

D. Working with a partner, choose three of the arguments from task C and, using what you learned in Academic Survival Skill (page 118), challenge the stated and unstated premises. Do the premises support the arguments? Why or why not?

1 ARGUMENT: _____

STATED PREMISE: _____

UNSTATED PREMISE: _____

SUPPORT THE ARGUMENT: ☐ YES ☐ NO

2 ARGUMENT: _____

STATED PREMISE: _____

UNSTATED PREMISE: _____

SUPPORT THE ARGUMENT: ☐ YES ☐ NO

3 ARGUMENT: _____

STATED PREMISE: _____

UNSTATED PREMISE: _____

SUPPORT THE ARGUMENT: ☐ YES ☐ NO

E. Read the following statements and indicate whether you think each one is true or false. For each false statement, write a true one.

STATEMENTS	TRUE	FALSE
1 The author equates intelligence in computers with her smartphone guiding her between locations. _____ _____		
2 Creativity is thought to be something that is restricted to humans, apes, and computers. _____ _____		
3 The aim of getting computers to do creative things is so far limited to having fun. _____ _____		
4 Accomplishing tasks like putting the right colours together in a picture shows that computers are advanced. _____ _____		

STATEMENTS	TRUE	FALSE
5 Examples of computer creativity include coming up with new recipes and new furniture designs. _____ _____		
6 Creativity is a concept that no one seems to be able to define. _____ _____		
7 Variety, divergence, and experimentation are three key aspects that contribute to creativity. _____ _____		
8 We have already reached a stage where people accept that computers are genuinely being creative in their own right. _____ _____		

F. So far, computers do not wake up in the morning and decide to paint a picture or write a novel. They need to be given a problem and the materials and programming to solve it. Does this lack of self-direction make computers more like factory workers than creative entities? Why or why not? In a small group, have half the members take one side of the argument and argue points in favour and have the other half take the opposite point of view and argue against it. Use what you learned in Academic Survival Skill to develop premises that support your point of view.

MyBookshelf > My eLab > Exercises > Chapter 5 > Can a Computer Be Creative?

FOCUS ON ACCURACY

Presenting Reasons, Causes, and Explanations

When presenting reasons, causes, and explanations, it is important to build arguments rather than simply list points. One way to do this is to explain a pre-existing fact or idea and segue (move) from it to the new point. You can use a connector such as *since* to help you.

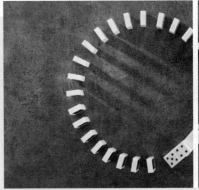

A. Consider these two examples from Listening 2. Work with a partner and rearrange the sentences so that *since* falls between the clauses rather than at the beginning.

1 And **since** that's kind of a cool story, the American science writer Carl Zimmer wrote about it, about how this poor fellow lost an ability that all of us have.

_____

_____

❷ Since words are kind of my medium if you will, my emotional medium, the thing with which I make things fixed in mind, I don't think that's weird at all.

_____

_____

B. Other connectors you can use include *as a result, because, consequently, due to,* and *so that.* Read the sentences and indicate with an arrow where the words in parentheses should go. Check your answers with a partner, saying each sentence aloud.

❶ (consequently) It's not just if you're like leaning on something in the environment and ↓ the idea is that you shouldn't have to really think about it in the cases where it's really working as part of the mental machinery .

❷ (as a result) That's not going to count partly because it takes ages to get down there and look it up and that resource just isn't there most of the time .

❸ (so that) Maybe it's emotionally enabling him to keep stuff at a distance he doesn't sort of jump to conclusions or rush to judgement .

❹ (due to) A lower court had ruled it was okay to inspect someone's iPhone when you arrest them the fact that it's something that exists within their physical space .

❺ (since) And we're deciding to visualize, there are also some connections to decision-making centres in the front of the brain .

❻ (because) This is a really difficult question for people to answer we don't actually have a definition of creativity that we can use to answer this question .

C. Work with a partner. Look at the illustrations below and take turns explaining what might have happened in each scenario, using *as a result, because, consequently, due to, since,* and *so that.* For example, you could describe the first picture as follows: *Because he wasn't holding onto the ladder, he fell.*

MyBookshelf > My eLab > Exercises > Chapter 5 > Accuracy Review

FINAL ASSIGNMENT
Take Part in a Creative Consultation

Now it's your turn. Use everything you have learned in this chapter to participate in a creative consultation of up to fifteen minutes. The point is to have participants take on different roles in sharing and discussing ideas.

A. Form a group of eight students and be ready to share the creative solution to the problem you chose in the Warm-Up Assignment (page 120).

B. Choose which pair speaks first, then assign one of the following roles to each of the other members of your group. After each pair presents, the other members not presenting switch roles. Consider making small signs defining each role that you can move from person to person as you discuss ideas.

- **DECISION-MAKER:** chairs the meeting, calling on others to speak
- **DREAMER:** asks hypothetical questions
- **REALIST:** considers costs and timelines
- **ANGEL'S ADVOCATE:** looks for additional benefits of new ideas
- **DEVIL'S ADVOCATE:** looks for shortcomings in new ideas
- **NOTE-TAKER:** summarizes and records ideas

Use what you learned in Focus on Critical Thinking (page 105) and Academic Survival Skill (page 118) to identify and evaluate problems and solutions.

C. Conduct your consultation meeting in front of the class; members of your group sit at a separate table and interact only with one another. Connect ideas using what you learned in Focus on Accuracy (page 125). The decision-maker needs to manage the time and ensure that everyone has a chance to speak. The note-taker may want to write ideas on the board. At the end of your meeting, invite questions or comments from the class.

D. Listen as other groups conduct their meetings. As each group speaks, use what you learned in Focus on Listening (page 104) to identify logical fallacies. Take notes and be prepared to ask questions.

E. Discuss the presentations as a class and evaluate which ones were the most successful at suggesting solutions to real-world problems. Which ones could have been more effective?

Critical Connections

In many countries around the world, a common problem is that students who start a post-secondary education program fail to graduate. There is no single cause to explain why many students drop out; for example, you may know students who have not succeeded in college or university because of poor study habits, unrealistic expectations, or lack of funds. What could be done to solve student dropout problems?

A. With a partner, use what you learned in Focus on Critical Thinking (page 105) to find reasons why students drop out. Could trial and error, algorithms, deductive or inductive reasoning, or heuristics (rules of thumb) be applied? Are there pros and cons?

B. Think of one or more approaches to the problem. For example, choose one reason why students drop out and provide a corresponding solution. Use what you learned in Focus on Speaking (page 112) and Academic Survival Skill to examine the premises and give examples. Use connectors you learned in Focus on Accuracy to help build your arguments.

C. Share your ideas in a group and use what you learned in Focus on Listening to identify logical fallacies. When everyone has finished, discuss the features of the best ideas. For example, are some ideas easier to implement, less expensive, or less time consuming?

CHAPTER 6
Rise of the Citizen Journalist

In 1883, the eruption of the Krakatoa volcano caused widespread destruction and the deaths of tens of thousands of people. Due to the recent spread of the telegraph to share news, this was one of the first major events ever reported around the world within hours of it happening. Since then, the speed and range of news travel have dramatically increased because of the actions of citizen journalists—unpaid people who capture news events in text, images, and video and share them on social media. Conversations are created when others follow up with diverse comments and opinions. What issues or events would make you want to become a citizen journalist?

In this chapter,
you will

- learn vocabulary about news gathering and sharing;

- listen to identify repair, qualification, and elaboration;

- evaluate speakers' motivations;

- consider ways to report speech;

- explore how to support arguments with research;

- adapt scientific reports to science podcasts;

- identify a scientific report and create a podcast.

GEARING UP

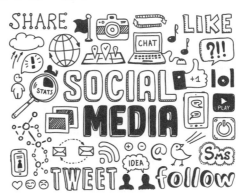

A. Look at the infographic and answer the questions.

① Countless people share news items they read on social media. What motivates people to share a particular story?

_____

_____

② To *like* a news story has become a way of voting for it, suggesting its importance to others. Are you influenced by how many *likes* a story has? Why or why not?

_____

_____

③ Tweets and other text messages are ways of making brief comments about a news story. Are word limits on tweets a problem or an advantage? Explain.

_____

_____

④ What is an example of a news story that you might follow? Why?

_____

_____

B. Compare your answers, first with a partner, then in a group. Choose the best answers.

Below are the key words you will practise in this chapter. Check the words you understand, then underline the words you use. Highlight the words you need to learn.

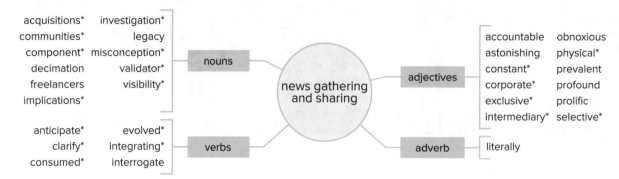

nouns

acquisitions* investigation*
communities* legacy
component* misconception*
decimation validator*
freelancers visibility*
implications*

verbs

anticipate* evolved*
clarify* integrating*
consumed* interrogate

news gathering and sharing

adjectives

accountable obnoxious
astonishing physical*
constant* prevalent
corporate* profound
exclusive* prolific
intermediary* selective*

adverb

literally

*Appears on the Academic Word List

FOCUS ON LISTENING

Listening for Repair, Qualification, and Elaboration

When you listen to a prepared speech, you expect that the speaker will not make mistakes and have to repair them, or need to back up to qualify or to elaborate. However, these three strategies are common in conversation and raise challenges for listeners.

Repair is a correction in which a speaker adjusts the information by changing a word, phrase, or sentence. A *qualification* is a statement that explains one or more exceptions to what is said. An elaboration adds information to make a speaker's message clearer. Often, these strategies begin with phrases that signal the type of correction that will be made.

A. Read the following examples of phrases that can be used with repair, qualification, and elaboration and add examples of your own. Compare your examples with those of a partner, practising sentences where you might use each one.

TECHNIQUE	EXAMPLE PHRASE	YOUR EXAMPLES
REPAIR	What I meant to say was, …	
QUALIFICATION	Although that doesn't include …	
ELABORATION	To explain that in more detail …	

B. In the following excerpt from Listening 1, note how the speaker, Kara Swisher, uses repair, qualification, and elaboration.

Mostly *is a qualification that says this is a reason for a preceding statement.*

Swisher begins by criticizing journalists for being negative and risk averse, then says that it's cynical for them to be so.

The word which *is used twice in this sentence, and signals elaboration. Swisher is explaining that she is a business journalist and* The (Wall Street) Journal *is a business publication.*

Swisher begins to say one thing, "And I walk," and then says it another way. She is repairing her statement.

> Mostly because journalists just literally are the most negative and risk-averse people on the planet. That's cynical—it's not even cynical, it's just stupid, like really, because they, you know, they sit around, and what's fascinating to me is I'm always saying journalists, business journalists which I am, and Raju works for *The Journal*, which is a business publication, many journalists who write about businesses have never run a business. They don't understand what's happening to their businesses. They don't understand what's happening at the profound level of media itself.
>
> And I walk—when I was walking out at *The Post*, Don is such a sweet guy came over and said, "Why are you leaving?" and I said, "The water's rising and you're on a lower floodplain than *The Wall Street Journal*."

Swisher repairs her use of the word cynical. *She then elaborates on what that means, saying that journalists are stupid.*

The words They don't understand … *are an elaboration on the idea of never having run a business. This is further elaborated in the next sentence, which begins the same way.*

C. Read the following sentences from Listening 1 and decide if each is an example of repair, qualification, or elaboration. Underline the part that introduces or shows each one.

1 So that's, I think, a very profound change in how we communicate and how readers communicate back with us, how our audiences communicate back. _____

2 There's never been a larger audience consuming journalism since, I would say, since 1450, since the Gutenberg press. _____

3 I think so there is a huge amount of like positive stuff that's happening driven by technology, driven by social media. _____

4 I mean the whole notion of church and state has become so ossified that you actually refuse to understand how business pays for your journalism. _____

FOCUS ON CRITICAL THINKING

Evaluating a Speaker's Motivations

If someone asks you if you have seen the news, you listen to understand what he or she is asking. But you also need to consider why the person is asking. For example, asking if someone has seen the news is usually a way of introducing a new topic about something in the news. The *why* question is about the speaker's motivation.

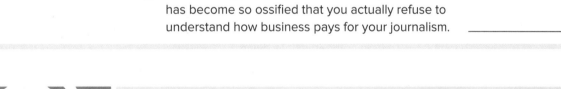

Trying to determine the motivation behind a person's words requires that you examine several factors. These include the speaker's background and experience, current position, and stated or unstated objectives, as well as the context in which the information is shared.

A. Read three excerpts from Listening 1 and answer the questions. As you do so, consider the speakers' motivations. Then discuss your answers with a partner to see if you share the same ideas.

1. It's also funny how *The Washington Post*'s saviour today is Jeff Bezos, who's made all his money on technology.

   a) The word *saviour* means "someone who rescues others from danger or difficulty." What point is the speaker making about Jeff Bezos and *The Washington Post*?

   _____

   _____

   b) Why do you think the speaker is making this point?

   _____

   _____

2. There's this whole canard that young people don't like quality content. It's just ridiculous. Young people are very smart. They love quality content. They're not a bunch of idiots.

   a) *Canard* (*duck*, in French) is slang for "unfounded rumour." What kind of audience do you expect this speaker is addressing?

   _____

   _____

   b) Why do you think the speaker is making this point?

   _____

   _____

3. One thing that's interesting about the sustainable business model part, the questions are coming from companies that actually probably don't have a sustainable business model anymore, right? Old media companies who question new media companies. We know the old media companies are dying.

   a) What point is the speaker making about old and new media?

   _____

   _____

   b) Why do you think the speaker is making this point?

   _____

   _____

   _____

B. Work in groups of three and each choose one of the following roles. Consider the motivations of the person you have chosen for your role, then discuss the three statements from that person's point of view.

• Traditional journalist who only works in newspapers

• Modern journalist who only works online

• Citizen journalist who sometimes reports on events

1. If we can stay on the cutting edge of technology and apply that technology to good and proper use, we can have an enormous impact on what we do and what we achieve with media.

2. We're not just consumers; we're producers. Indeed, we all have the ability to be journalists and publishers.

3. The Internet is also a marketplace where consumers have dramatically different expectations. They are no longer the passive audience, respectfully absorbing what mainstream wants to tell them.

C. After, discuss how playing the roles changed your perceptions of the statements.

LISTENING 1

VIDEO

The Future of Journalism: Old Media Is Dying

In 2017, the *Buenos Aires Herald* newspaper closed after 140 years of operation. It's a story that is being repeated around the world as print media organizations struggle to compete with digital services. Is digital the future of the news?

VOCABULARY BUILD

In the following exercises, explore key words from Listening 1.

A. For each of the following key words, identify the root word. Then, with a partner, explain the differences between the root word and the key word.

KEY WORD	ROOT WORD	DIFFERENCES
1. acquisitions	*acquire*	Acquisitions *are things you get;* acquire *is a verb that means to "get something."*
2. implications		
3. integrating		
4. literally		
5. selective		

B. Choose the correct word in parentheses to complete each sentence, based on the context suggested by the key word in bold.

1. The **decimation** of newspapers is about their (birth / growth / death).

2. A **profound** change in newspapers has to do with their (digitization / printing / photos).

3. Increasingly, people find (negative / positive / neutral) online comments on stories to be **obnoxious**.

4. Newspapers have **evolved**, that is to say, they have (never / slowly / immediately) changed.

5. An **astonishing** feature of citizen journalists is that so many work (for salaries / as professionals / for free).

C. The word *literally* is usually contrasted with *figuratively* or *metaphorically*. A metaphorical expression is one that is not meant to be taken as fact. However, speakers often confuse the use of these expressions. Read the following two sentences from Listening 1 and decide if the speaker is using *literally* correctly. Discuss your answer with a partner.

1. Journalists *literally* are the most negative and risk-averse people on the planet.

2. The reporters were *literally* just as obnoxious as the industry they were covering.

Before You Listen

A. Read an excerpt from B. Raju Narisetti, taken from Listening 1. Then answer the questions. After, share your answers with a partner and discuss any answers you disagree about.

The second thing to remember: oftentimes, there's a lot of a gloom and doom about what's happening in the journalism world, but the reality is that there's never been a larger audience consuming journalism since, I would say, since 1450, since the Gutenberg press. I mean Kara today is probably heard, read, and engaged with by more people today than ever before in all our journalism years.

Gutenberg's printing press

1. What is Narisetti referring to when he mentions "doom and gloom in journalism"?

_____

_____

② The Gutenberg press was the first European press for printing books. It changed the nature of learning by making inexpensive books widely available. In what ways was this invention both similar to and different from the introduction of the Internet?

_____

_____

_____

③ Narisetti says that the journalist (Kara Swisher) is "probably heard, read, and engaged with by more people today than ever before in all our journalism years." Why do you think this is so?

_____

_____

_____

B. The term *echo chamber* is used to describe a conversation among people who share the same backgrounds and motivations and who are, therefore, likely to share the same opinions and be less open to new ideas. Read the brief biographies of the three speakers in Listening 1. With a partner, make a few notes about the background of another person who might provide a different point of view.

- **John Kennedy** is a technology journalist and editor at *Silicon Republic,* a technology news website.

- **B. Raju Narisetti**, Senior Vice-President, Strategy, for News Corporation, had previously been Managing Editor of *The Wall Street Journal Digital Network.*

- **Kara Swisher**, technology journalist and co-founder of *Recode* (an online news site), had previously written for *The Wall Street Journal.*

FOURTH SPEAKER'S BACKGROUND: _____

_____

_____

C. Part of the focus of the discussion is on a company called Storyful that keeps an eye on social media and quickly licenses citizen journalist videos. Why might this be a useful service for online news websites? Discuss with a partner, then check your answer as you listen.

_____

_____

While You Listen

D. As you watch and listen to Part 1 of the video, use what you learned in Focus on Listening (page 130) to identify when the speakers repair, qualify, and elaborate on what they have to say. Then answer the questions.

KEY POINTS AND QUESTIONS	ANSWERS
1 **John Kennedy:** I suppose, to begin with, twenty years ago … WHAT IS KENNEDY'S MOTIVATION IN TELLING THE STORY OF WHAT REPORTING USED TO BE LIKE?	
2 **B. Raju Narisetti:** I went the journalism school like thousand years ago, and … WHAT DOES NARISETTI ELABORATE ON?	
3 **Narisetti:** I think so there is a huge amount of like positive stuff that's happening driven by technology, driven by social media, that's sometimes lost in kind of all … WHAT POINT IS REPAIRED?	
4 **Kara Swisher:** Mostly because journalists just literally are the most negative and risk-averse people on the planet.	*discussed in Focus on Listening*
5 **Swisher:** • … when I left to go to *The Wall Street Journal,* • Don Graham … stopped me when I was going to *The Wall Street Journal,* … • … and when I walked out of *The Washington Post,* Don Graham's like, "Why are you leaving?" • And I walk, when I was walking out at *The Post,* Don is such a sweet guy came over and said, "Why are you leaving?" WHAT POINT IS SHE MAKING WITH HER REPAIRS?	
6 **Kennedy:** … so basically they're also making forays into basically how the structure of publishing as we know it's going to be for the next … IN HIS REPAIR, WHAT DOES KENNEDY USE AS A METAPHOR FOR THE STRUCTURE OF THE INTERNET?	
7 **Narisetti:** We try to engage people on Facebook, … WHAT QUALIFICATION DOES NARISETTI MAKE ABOUT *THE WALL STREET JOURNAL*?	
8 **Swisher:** You know, nobody like goes like this, nobody goes to the store and says, "I would like the crappy meat, please." WHAT POINT IS SWISHER TRYING TO MAKE AS SHE REPAIRS HER STATEMENTS AND ELABORATES ON HER METAPHOR?	
9 **Narisetti:** Actually, radio, as you know, is one of the most seamless ways … WHAT POINT IS NARISETTI MAKING AS HE REFERS TO AR, VR, AND DRIVERLESS CARS?	
10 **Swisher:** And, by the way, driverless cars it's 2 percent now, but it's gonna be 100 percent. WHAT IS SWISHER'S ELABORATION ABOUT?	

E. Now watch Part 2 of the video and take notes on a separate page. You will use your notes to answer the questions in task F.

After You Listen

F. Check your comprehension by answering these questions with a partner. Once you have finished, meet with another pair of students to compare and choose the best answers.

1 When Kennedy says, "The silver lining I see inside is that storytelling can get richer," what does he mean?

_____

_____

2 Kennedy says, "When I think about the future of media, I think about recent acquisitions ..." What does he mean by *acquisitions*?

_____

_____

3 What is Kennedy referring to when he asks, "And what about the seismic shifts we're gonna see in terms of ownership?"

_____

_____

4 The word *hubris* means excessive pride and self-confidence. When Narisetti uses *hubris* to describe traditional news publishers, what does he mean?

_____

_____

5 When Narisetti says, "There's a belief that there's a lot of content that's going to be generated by ... people with phones, because they can," what is his point?

_____

_____

6 In Narisetti's comment, "Verifying is a big aspect of it," what is meant by *verifying*; what does it involve?

_____

_____

7 Narisetti says, "And then, finally, the whole notion of licensing." What does he mean by *licensing*?

_____

_____

G. Narisetti talks about how new media companies can "engage and retain and grow audiences in a very rapid way and kind of bring down the average age of the audience in a big way, as well." With a partner, discuss how a news site aimed at people your age does each of these things:

1 Engage readers/viewers. _____

2 Retain and grow audiences. _____

H. Why has commenting on web-based articles become so popular? Discuss your answers in a group.

_____

_____

FOCUS ON ACCURACY

Reporting Speech

There are two ways to report speech. The first is to simply state who is speaking and repeat his or her words. The second, more common, way is to add a point of view about what the person says.

A. Although you can just mention that someone said something and repeat the exact words, there are also particular techniques and phrases you can use to report speech. Fill in the Reported Speech column in the table, changing the tenses in the Direct Speech column as indicated. After, check your answers with a partner.

DIRECT SPEECH	TENSE CHANGE	REPORTED SPEECH
I am a reporter.	simple present → simple past*	*She said (that) she was a reporter.* *
I am recording podcasts.	present progressive → past progressive	*She mentioned*
I worked at a magazine before.	simple past → past perfect	*She told us*
I was reporting on the computer industry.	past progressive → past perfect progressive	*She said*
I haven't lost my love of magazines.	present perfect → past perfect	*She explained*
But I had taken a year off after I quit.	past perfect (no change)	*She remarked*
I will never go back to analog media.	simple future *will* → *would*	*She commented*

*In spoken language, the simple present tense can be used if the event just happened:
  She says (that) she's a reporter.

With modals like *could, may, might, should,* and *would,* use the same word as in direct speech:

> I *would* like to win a podcasting award. → She said that she *would* like to win a podcasting award.

An exception is the modal *can.* Change *can* to *could* in reported speech.

> I *can* do it if I try. → She said she *could* do it if she tried.

B. There are many ways to add a point of view when reporting another person's speech. Consider the following brief exchange, adapted from Listening 2. With a partner, discuss three ways the exchange could be reported, for example, starting with a comment such as, *You wouldn't believe it but* ... or *He seems to think that* ... How do the added phrases influence the meaning?

> Host: How are we defining citizen journalists?
> Adams: They're ordinary people who are not professional journalists.

C. With a partner, practise sentences related to citizen journalists. After you say sample sentence 1, your partner turns what you said into reported speech as in sample sentence 2. Take turns, and check each other's sentences.

Example:

1 Next year, I will be a citizen journalist and capture news on my phone's video camera.

2 She mentioned that next year she would be a citizen journalist and capture news on her phone's video camera.

MyBookshelf > My eLab > Exercises > Chapter 6 > Accuracy Review

MyBookshelf > My eLab > Exercises > Chapter 6 > Accuracy Review

LISTENING ❷ How to Be a Citizen Journalist

It is easy to become a citizen journalist by simply being in the right place at the right time, for example, capturing photos or video of a disaster or an important historical moment, and sharing your observations online. But if you want to be a citizen journalist to explore issues you care about, what tools and training might help you succeed?

VOCABULARY BUILD

In the following exercises, explore key words from Listening 2.

A. Studying the origins of words (their etymologies) can help to understand their meanings. Look at the following key words in bold and answer the questions.

1 The word **freelancers** was first used to describe fighters who could be hired for battle; their spears, called *lances*, were *free*, or available. Why do you think the word has come to be used for people who work on short-term jobs?

_____

_____

2 The word **interrogate** is made up of the prefix *inter*, meaning *between*, and the verb *rogare*, meaning *ask*. How do these two definitions help you understand the meaning *interrogate*?

_____

_____

③ The word **anticipate** is from the Latin words *ante*, meaning "before," and *capere*, meaning "take." What does *anticipate* mean?

_____

_____

④ The word **validator** is related to *validate*, which originally meant "make something legal." The meaning is similar today, but the *–or* suffix changes the verb into a noun, referring to a person who validates. Which other words in this Vocabulary Build could have an *–or* or *–er* suffix added to make them refer to people?

_____

_____

⑤ The word **corporate** comes from the Latin word *corpus*, which means "body." Why might we describe a business as a body?

_____

_____

B. When you learn new words, take the time to learn words that are related to them in some way; they can be either similar or opposite in meaning. For each of the following key words, choose three related words from the word box. After, with a partner, practise making sentences about journalism using these words.

constituent	middleman	parties	populations	unclear
go-between	murky	people	prominence	unknown
invisible	part	perception	societies	~~whole~~

① component _____*whole*_____ _____ _____

② communities _____ _____ _____

③ intermediary _____ _____ _____

④ clarify _____ _____ _____

⑤ visibility _____ _____ _____

C. The term *communities* has a particular meaning in Listening 2. It refers to the groups, such as teams, clubs, and social organizations, to which people belong. Besides your university community, think of three other communities you are part of. Then, in a group, discuss what belonging to each of them involves in terms of your rights and responsibilities.

_____ _____ _____

Before You Listen

A. Read an excerpt from Listening 2. Think about a community you or someone you know belongs to and a newsworthy issue of concern to that group. Discuss your answers with a partner.

> So, we're just talking about ordinary people who are not professional journalists who want to get involved with telling stories in their communities. And when I say communities, I don't mean just, you know, your geographic community. Like, I live in Sandy Hill, but maybe that too, but also, in an artistic community, in a sports community, in a community of interest. So, we think that there's space now on the Web for people, ordinary people to give voice, right? And one of the things that I can do as a journalism educator is provide people with some of the tools that we give journalism students and that journalists use in their everyday work. So, that's the idea.

MY COMMUNITY: _____

AN ISSUE THAT OTHERS SHOULD LEARN ABOUT: _____

B. The speaker in Listening 2, Paul Adams, is a former journalist and professor at Carleton University's School of Journalism and Communication. He teaches students who are aiming to become full-time professional journalists. Why do you think he's also interested in teaching part-time citizen journalists? Think of three reasons. Then share your answers with a partner and choose the best three.

1 _____

2 _____

3 _____

While You Listen

C. Listen once to get the general idea about the questions the interviewer is asking. Listen again to complete the notes on Adams's responses.

INTERVIEWER QUESTIONS	ADAMS'S RESPONSES
1 Because certainly, there's no shortage of people blogging and posting things all the time. It doesn't always necessarily follow journalistic guidelines necessarily. And certainly, even the idea of figuring out what a story is and how to tell those stories. What are some of the things that people may be overlooking when they're thinking, well, what do I need to know?	• *One of the big challenges is coming up with* • *Citizen journalists are different because* • *There's a worry that citizen journalists don't have any standards or ethics, and don't*
2 We went to school for this.	• *It's not citizen journalists who take jobs away from journalists, it's*
3 Is part of it—I mean, this is interesting because when we still could afford freelancers …*	• *Freelancers had stories that*
4 How do you—I wonder whether you talk much during that—in the course, of looking for stories that aren't your own.	• *Citizen journalists want to find ways to tell stories about* • *You get a more balanced*

INTERVIEWER QUESTIONS	ADAMS'S RESPONSES
5 The flipside of that also that I find sometimes when I'm doing events where people brush off stories that they think, oh, that's probably not that interesting, probably, you guys, this wouldn't actually be that interesting. I often say to people, no, that's actually a really interesting story, what is happening and you guys—this is, we just have to find a way to tell it or find the right characters within it. What is an example of something that people might not immediately recognize as a great story that could be one?	• *The bicycle lanes are successful but there are conflicts between* • *Some stories aren't as interesting to the general public, but you can connect with them on*
6 This brings up an interesting question because sometimes I think there—I will sometimes stumble across a blog or somebody online who's putting out quite interesting stories that tell—and I wonder, how many people are really reading this? And the readership is fairly small. Is—you mentioned your hopes for the future where citizen journalism will start being paid or subsidized by non-profits, etc. For people who may feel somewhat daunted by the fact, well yeah, I could put this great story out there, who the heck is ever going to see it? What do you tell them?	• *Citizen journalists do not want to be* • *Citizen journalists couldn't connect fifteen years ago with*
7 But even within controlled subject matter, right?	*Right.*
8 Like, there's so many now that it gets harder and harder. You know, I think that it gets harder and harder for people to nab a little bit of—	• *One of the functions of something like Apt613 is you can anticipate a certain quality of* • *Apt613 wants to be a little bigger and better than* • *There is a thirst for information and increasingly, newspapers*

After You Listen

D. The role of an interviewer is to prompt the interviewee to talk. But what are the motivations behind the interviewer's questions or comments? With a partner, use what you learned in Focus on Critical Thinking (page 131) to discuss the following comments made by the interviewer in Listening 2. Consider the interviewer's motivation in each one, then explain it below.

1 We went to school for this.

_____

_____

2 The flipside of that, also that I find sometimes when I'm doing events where people brush off stories that they think, oh, that's probably not that interesting.

_____

_____

_____

3 I wonder, how many people are really reading this? And the readership is fairly small.

_____

_____

> *Some questions are statements; they act as prompts to encourage the interviewee to address a topic.*

E. Read the following statements and indicate whether you think each one is true or false. For each false statement, write a true one.

STATEMENTS	TRUE	FALSE
❶ Citizen journalism is a way to ensure that local issues have greater visibility.		
❷ Large media companies are starting to focus on a lot of smaller places.		
❸ People who are blogging and posting things all the time tend to follow journalistic guidelines.		
❹ Major media outlets use freelancers more often than ever before.		
❺ The idea of interrogating documents and websites refers to evaluating them carefully.		
❻ The Internet allows you to tell a story for a smaller or a more selective community.		
❼ Most bloggers want to become like *The New York Times*.		
❽ Increasingly, newspapers aren't filling people's need for news about particular topics of interest to them.		

F. On Twitter, Facebook, and other social media, everyone can be a citizen journalist. People can report news in the form of stories, photos, audios, and videos, and also share their opinions. If you wanted to become a citizen journalist, what skills might help you become effective?

❶ _____

❷ _____

❸ _____

❹ _____

❺ _____

MyBookshelf > My eLab >
Exercises > Chapter 6 >
How to Be a Citizen Journalist

Supporting Arguments with Research

Throughout university and perhaps during your career, you will often be asked to share news about research, summarizing key points and explaining their significance. The research may be from your own or others' work. The most important part of discussing research is knowing when to mention specific data about the findings or results of the research and how to present or explain it.

Generally, you don't need to support your ideas with research when information is common knowledge. But when the information is new for your listeners, you may need to provide evidence. This evidence is likely to include results, conclusions, and implications.

A. Review the following purposes for sharing ideas about research. Add one or more phrases to each row in the second column.

PURPOSES	EXAMPLE PHRASES
INTRODUCE A TOPIC	• This study looked at ... • Beginning with the research question ..., this study explored ... •
INDICATE A PROBLEM OR A GAP IN KNOWLEDGE ON THE TOPIC	• This question has not been researched much in the past. • Previous research focused on ... instead of ... •
SHARE INFORMATION THAT IS NOT COMMON KNOWLEDGE	• According to Adams, ... • As Adams suggests, ... •
SHARE A SPECIFIC SUPPORTING POINT	• A key point is ... • As an example, • For example, • For instance, • That is, •
STATE EXCEPTIONS	• However, something different is ... • An exception is ... • Something that doesn't fit is ... •
REPORT RESULTS FROM INTERVIEWS, QUESTIONNAIRES, AND SURVEYS	• Of the 300 subjects, 72 percent ... • The response rate for the survey was 56 percent. • The majority of respondents felt ... •
EXPLAIN IMPORTANCE	• The importance of this study is ... • The reasons this study makes a difference are ... •

Use "such as" to introduce a specific example that is part of a category. Use "like" if a point is similar, but not part of the topic.

B. Read the following title and abstract on citizen journalism. Use what you learned in the table in task A to discuss it with a partner. Be sure to use one or more examples from each of the purposes. After you have practised, pair up with other partners and try again.

Editorial Gatekeeping in Citizen Journalism

Editorial staff play an essential role as gatekeepers within professional journalism. Citizen journalism has the potential to depart from routine journalistic practices and allow for more democratic posting of unmoderated content. Nonetheless, many citizen journalism websites do have an editorial staff, and no existing research has explored the contributions of editors to citizen journalism websites. I theorize that the editorial staff on citizen journalism sites serve as *legitimating organizational structure*s within the larger organizational field and as *citizen gatekeepers*, who enforce journalistic routines. Using a content analysis of a sample (n=326) drawn from the largest sampling frame of English-language citizen journalism websites based in the United States to date (n=1958), I examine the characteristics of citizen journalism websites with an editorial model as well as how the presence of an editorial staff is associated with the practice of journalistic routines common in professional journalism.

Lindner, A. M. (2016, February 22). Editorial gatekeeping in citizen journalism. *New Media and Society.* Retrieved from http://journals.sagepub.com/doi/abs/10.1177/1461444816631506

MyBookshelf > My eLab > Exercises > Chapter 6 > Focus on Speaking

Academic
Survival Skill

Adapting Scientific Reports to Science Podcasts

News stories often rewrite reports from scientific journals to make them easier to understand by the general public; one example is in podcasts.

Research-based scientific reports include the following sections. Compare the purpose of each section with the section in a podcast.

SECTIONS	PURPOSE OF THE SECTIONS IN A SCIENTIFIC REPORT	PURPOSE OF THE SECTIONS IN A PODCAST OF A SCIENTIFIC ARTICLE
TITLE	Identify one or more key questions or ideas.	Attract the listener's attention.
ABSTRACT	Summarize the hypothesis and the research questions.	None
INTRODUCTION	Outline the background of the study.	Identify the key research questions or idea and perhaps give background.
METHOD	Explain how evidence was gathered.	Explain how evidence was gathered.
RESULTS	Show the data that was collected.	Explain the results.
DISCUSSION	Explore how the method helped answer the research questions and proved or disproved the hypothesis.	Explain the significance of the results.
REFERENCES	List sources cited in the text.	None
APPENDICES	List extra information about the study that is too detailed to go in the body of the article.	None

A. Read an abstract of a scientific article and answer the questions about how you might adapt the findings to a podcast.

> **Sweat So You Don't Forget: Exercise Breaks during a University Lecture Increase On-Task Attention and Learning**
>
> We examined the impact of taking exercise breaks, non-exercise breaks, or no breaks on learning among first-year Introductory Psychology students. Three 5-minute breaks were equally distributed throughout a 50-minute computer-based video lecture. The exercise breaks group performed a series of callisthenic exercises; the non-exercise breaks group played a computer game; the no breaks group watched the lecture without breaks. Mind-wandering questions measured attention during the lecture. Exercise breaks promoted attention throughout the lecture compared to no breaks and non-exercise breaks, and resulted in superior learning when assessed on immediate and delayed tests. The exercise breaks group also endorsed higher ratings for narrator clarity and perceived understanding than the other two groups. This is the first study to show that exercise breaks promote attention during lecture and improve learning in university students.
>
> Fenesi, B., Lucibello, K. Heisz, J. J., & Kim, J. A. (2018, June). Sweat so you don't forget: Exercise breaks during a university lecture increase on-task attention and learning. *Journal of Applied Research in Memory and Cognition, 7*(2), 261–269. doi:10.1016/j.jarmac.2018.01.012

1 Traditionally, scientific articles used the passive voice. But this is now changing and use of the active voice is common. For example, this abstract begins with a first-person plural subject. How would you rewrite the first sentence in the passive voice, omitting *we*?

_____

_____

2 The title is conversational. Which of the following would be a more scientific version?

a) Sweating and Remembering: Exercise Breaks during a University Lecture Increase On-Task Attention and Learning

b) Sweat So You Remember: Exercising Breaks Up University Lectures and Increases On-Task Attention and Learning

c) Exercise Breaks during a University Lecture Increase On-Task Attention and Learning

3 What would be a good short title for a podcast to attract listeners' attention? It could be posed as a question.

_____

4 Explaining the method would usually start by introducing the researchers and saying something about them. Assume this has been done and summarize the method in two or three sentences, outlining the most important points.

_____

_____

_____

⑤ What were the results? Explain them in one sentence.

_____

⑥ It is likely that the study is useful generally, not only for psychology students. Based on what you understand from the abstract, explain how the results could be useful for everyone.

_____

_____

_____

Many news items, such as podcasts, are presented in what is called the inverted pyramid structure. Key information (the results) is presented first, and less important information (method and discussion) and background details after. This format allows your listeners to get the gist of the story and then decide whether or not they are interested enough to learn the details. The final sentences, however, may make a dramatic or memorable point.

❶ You can cut inverted pyramid stories from the bottom up, if less important information doesn't fit the time available.

B. Read details from a news story about a company that licenses social media videos. Number the sections to put them in an inverted pyramid format, from most (1) to least (4) important details. Compare your answers with a partner.

• Level _____ Storyful now has offices in Dublin, New York, and Hong Kong.

• Level _____ Storyful, a media licensing company based in Ireland, shares research that user-generated content is 35 percent more memorable than traditional brand creative videos.

• Level _____ What do you think is better? A million-dollar sleek corporate video or a silly video badly shot on someone's mobile phone? The answer turns out to be the latter.

• Level _____ Since 2010, when it was started by Irish journalist Mark Little, Storyful has been making it easier for citizen reporters to make money from their videos. However, Storyful's main clients are news organizations that want to use social media but need to be sure they have licensing rights to new videos.

WARM-UP ASSIGNMENT
Identify a Scientific Report to Adapt as a Podcast

Whatever university discipline you are in or planning to enter, it's likely that there are scientific reports written about it, published as journal articles. Researching these articles helps you understand your subject. Converting the information to podcasts can help you share and remember it.

Visit My eLab
Documents to learn
more about citation and
referencing guidelines.

A. Choose a recent journal article in your field that you find interesting. You may want to search through journals in the library or look online; use key words related to your discipline and areas of interest, plus the words *scientific report* or *journal article*. Keep complete records of your source, following the citation and referencing guidelines of your discipline.

B. Use what you learned in Academic Survival Skill (page 145) to review the abstract and identify the key points:

SECTIONS	YOUR SCIENTIFIC ARTICLE: SUMMARY POINTS
TITLE	
ABSTRACT	
INTRODUCTION	
METHOD	
RESULTS	
DISCUSSION	

C. Consider the writer's motivation, based on what you learned in Focus on Critical Thinking (page 131). Why is the topic being investigated? How is it important? Will the results lead to an improvement or change of some kind?

D. Use the inverted pyramid structure you learned in Academic Survival Skill to organize your notes. Think of a dramatic final statement to inspire the audience. It could be a comment, a question, or a suggestion for action— something your listeners should consider doing.

E. Use your notes to write a three- to five-minute script, including supporting details; you don't need to write every word but make sure to present the key points. Use what you learned in Focus on Speaking (page 144) to discus research.

F. Practise your script with a partner, discussing how you can improve the content and delivery of your news coverage of the scientific report. Keep your notes for your Final Assignment, when you will record your audio or video podcast, perhaps using your mobile phone.

Use feedback from
your teacher and
classmates on this
Warm-Up Assignment
to improve your notes.

LISTENING ③

The Evolution of Journalism and Tapping into Tech for Storytelling

Since the first website was created in 1991, the Internet has competed with newspapers and other media for readers' attention. Lianna Brinded explores issues around how people today want to get their news and how print media continue to be perceived as more legitimate than digital sources.

VOCABULARY BUILD

In the following exercises, explore key words from Listening 3.

A. With a partner, discuss the meaning of the words in bold, based on the contexts. Then, write your own paraphrase of each sentence, replacing the key word with a synonym. Highlight the synonym and then share your paraphrased sentences with your partner.

① Identify who the readers are, what platforms they read on, and how best to display, and also write in a way the story is **accountable** to that subject.

_____

② There's still that **legacy** issue that print is more valuable and online isn't.

_____

③ That's been something that's been really, you know, **prevalent** over the last few years.

_____

④ Online journalism still has that **misconception** that a lot of it is not valuable because it's a lot more sloppy.

_____

⑤ Clickbait has been quite **prolific** and actually has been an example of why online journalism isn't as prestigious as print.

_____

B. For each of the following key words, write at least two common collocations. Then work with a partner and come up with sentences related to journalism using each key word and one or more collocations.

① constant _____

② consumed _____

③ exclusive _____

④ investigation _____

⑤ physical _____

MyBookshelf > My eLab >
Exercises > Chapter 6 >
Vocabulary Review

Before You Listen

A. Read an excerpt from Listening 3 and answer the questions. After, compare answers with a partner to see where you agree and disagree.

> I've been working in online journalism for a while but if I get an article in print, my Mum will still go to me, "Oh well done, that's great" and I'm like but how about all the other hundreds of million articles that I've written on other things that, you know, one million people have read, it's more like, "Oh that's nice, I can keep it and print it out."

1 Why do you think the mother prefers the printed articles to online ones?

_____

_____

2 The mother values print journalism more than online journalism. Do you feel the same way? Why or why not?

_____

_____

3 One focus of Brinded's talk is about the move to mobile as the dominant platform for reading news. How might this affect the mother's appreciation of online journalism?

_____

_____

_____

_____

B. In general, use of smartphones is increasing not only for online journalism but also for Internet access. Why? Think of three reasons and compare answers with a partner. Then choose the best ones.

1 _____

2 _____

3 _____

While You Listen

C. Listen once to fill in details about the talk, then listen again and use what you learned in Focus on Speaking (page 144) to try to identify the purpose the speaker has for mentioning each point (use the numbers to indicate each one):

1 Introduce a topic

2 Indicate a problem or a gap in knowledge on the topic

3 Share information that is not common knowledge

4 Share a specific supporting point

5 State exceptions

6 Report results from interviews, questionnaires, and surveys

7 Explain importance

> **!** MO refers to modus operandi and refers to a way of doing things.

LECTURE POINTS	DETAILS AND PURPOSES
1 But the thing is, people hate clickbait and ...	*used as an example of why* PURPOSE: _____
2 You've had people that, you know, instead of doing an article, ...	*it'll just be constant slide shows, or it will be tricking the reader into clicking more, and people are* PURPOSE: _____
3 On top of that we've got fake news, the spread of misinformation.	*while it's been great in terms of speed and how we get our information* PURPOSE: __7__
4 It's not as fine-tuned as something in *The New York Times* print or *Washington Post* or *Wall Street Journal* where, you know, there may be hours of, you know well, ...	*perceptions of* PURPOSE: _____
5 And that's again, damaging the online brand but now we are at a point where online journalism, ...	*digital journalism has tried lots of different things and some things* PURPOSE: _____
6 What we want to do is, we want to be trustworthy, we want to get a message out, a story, an investigation or ...	*relaying some very important information to the masses and* PURPOSE: _____
7 You want to kill this clickbait and curiosity gaps and you want to get back to storytelling.	*and using* PURPOSE: _____
8 But really, it's different online, you've got to ask yourself, "Where are you providing the value for the reader?" We're going to print it on a piece of paper, ...	*where it's like, we don't know* PURPOSE: _____
9 So, for instance, we have on this chart we made in-house called *Atlas*, which is open source—anyone can use it— ...	*but so the mobile Internet is* PURPOSE: _____
10 We forget that we spend a lot of time on home pages, on online, we think that websites are the be all and end all.	*but actually most of the Internet is* PURPOSE: _____
11 Same with the tablet. Obviously there's lots of companies out there that have media outlets that do tablet-only, ...	*is it worth spending those millions or your time as well trying to develop ways* PURPOSE: _____
12 "Do I need to write one thousand words on that story?" ...	*or can you have that killer chart with a bit of context that ...* PURPOSE: _____
13 But we have found that adoption in readers, there's that kind of dead zone.	*where it's like, you know,* PURPOSE: _____

After You Listen

D. Discuss the key points of the lecture with a partner, then write your own summary. Compare summaries with your partner and, together, write a final version.

_____

_____

_____

_____

_____

E. Read the questions and choose the best answers.

1. The speaker says that both Facebook and Google are punishing media outlets that use clickbait. What reasons might they have for doing so?

   a) It's likely that clickbait journalism gives sites like Facebook and Google a bad name among news consumers.

   b) Almost everyone who follows clickbait webpages is likely to end up on a competing website.

   c) Most people prefer to only read clickbait stories when they know they are entertainment, not news.

2. The speaker talks about fake news in terms of the spread of misinformation and the speed at which we get our information. How might the two be related?

   a) Information spreads quickly if it is both true and important; you are more likely to get fake news from print media.

   b) Misinformation is often called fake news by those who don't believe in it and are upset at not being able to share it quickly enough.

   c) Because of the public's interest in getting online news as quickly as possible, it's likely that fake news stories are shared before they are verified.

3. The speaker suggests that what online journalists want is to be trustworthy. What steps are necessary for online journalism to become trustworthy?

   a) She suggests that no one is likely to trust online journalism unless he or she can compare stories to more trusted print media sources.

   b) She believes that it is best to start with stories from print sources such as _The New York Times_ to increase people's trust.

   c) She thinks journalists should share a message, a story, or an investigation with the public and give reasons why people should read it.

4. The speaker suggests that governments will often use fear as a motivating force to convince their populations that Internet restrictions are necessary. How might governments do this?

   a) They can force people to use parental controls to stop children from seeing inappropriate content.

   b) They might suggest that foreign countries are using the Internet for propaganda that needs to be blocked.

   c) They can make their own websites to promote their values and encourage people to look at them.

5 The speaker discusses word length when writing news stories. What is the purpose of writing stories that range from around five hundred to a thousand words?

a) This length likely matches readers' limited attention spans, particularly when they are looking at news on mobile devices.

b) She explains that if online journalists want to be taken seriously, they need to be writing more than they would for print media.

c) She is warning readers against looking at stories that are too long or too short to be meaningful.

6 Why does the speaker raise the question, "Where are you providing the value for the reader?" in relation to online journalism?

a) It's important for online journalism to try hard to follow the lead of print journalism in addressing readers' traditional needs.

b) It's important to ensure that online journalism takes advantage of mobile phones and other devices to better serve readers.

c) It's important for the growth of print media like newspapers and magazines to have online versions for customers who prefer them.

7 What concern is the speaker addressing when she discusses using "killer charts" in online journalism.

a) She's suggesting that it's sometimes better to use a concise chart to share the information rather than hundreds of words.

b) She realizes that people would rather look at charts than read because they do not have to scroll through several paragraphs.

c) She realizes that while print media sometimes use charts, they cannot make them animated the way mobile journalism can.

8 What is the purpose of the speaker's story about writing a long story and then deciding that it would be more effective to tell it in fewer words?

a) She is trying to explain that it is often better to tell several shorter stories rather than focus your attention on one longer one.

b) She is emphasizing the need to consider readers' interest in the topic and whether a short or long form is justified.

c) She is introducing the idea that fewer words are necessary when the online journalist cannot think of what else to say.

F. After listening, what details are you most likely to remember about online journalism? Share them with a partner and discuss why they are memorable.

MyBookshelf > My eLab >
Exercises > Chapter 6 >
The Evolution of Journalism

FINAL ASSIGNMENT
Create a Podcast Based on a Scientific Report

Now it's your turn. Use everything you have learned in this chapter to edit, then produce and share the content of your audio or video podcast. Be prepared to answer questions about it from other students.

A. Revisit the podcast notes you created for your Warm-Up Assignment (page 147). Make sure you have used what you learned in Academic Survival Skill (page 145) and Focus on Speaking (page 144) to explain key points about your scientific report. Using what you learned in Focus on Critical Thinking (page 131), consider your own motivation in sharing your information. Why does it interest you? What is your point of view on the content? How do you make that clear to your audience?

B. Share your podcast with your group. In your role as an expert, be prepared to answer questions, using what you learned in Focus on Speaking to discuss scientific issues. Review the repair, clarification, and elaboration strategies from Focus on Listening (page 130) to help overcome any problems you have in making your answers clear.

C. As you listen to other students' podcasts, ask probing questions to find out more details about important points.

D. After, reflect with your group members on what went well and what could be improved, and decide what you should review.

Critical Connections

Before the arrival of social media, reporters were highly accountable for the news that they reported. Making a mistake or sharing fake news could cost them their jobs. Fake news is common on social media partly because the cost of entry is so low—you don't need to start a newspaper or television station to share your views. However, fake news is also common because people who share it online can be difficult to identify so they don't always feel accountable.

A. In a group, consider these three types of fake news. Try to think of at least one example of each type.

- FAKE MEDICAL NEWS: promising so-called miracle cures or suggesting that legitimate scientifically proven cures do not work

- FAKE POLITICAL NEWS: promoting or criticizing a particular candidate or cause

- FAKE SOCIAL NEWS: attacking certain groups in society or government programs

B. For each fake news story you identify (or type of story if you cannot find examples), use what you learned in Focus on Critical Thinking (page 131) to examine the motivation of the speakers who spread it. Use the mind map to fill in your answers. Share your ideas in a group.

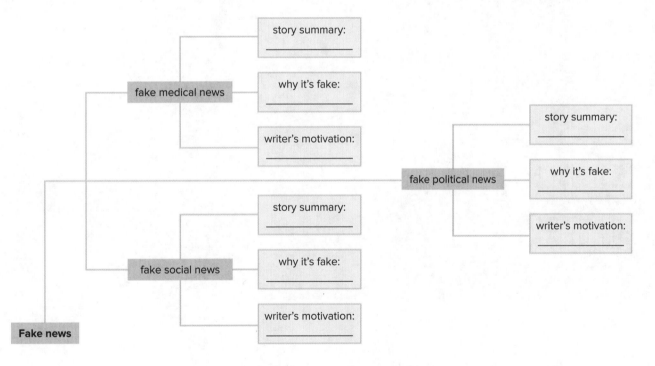

C. On your own, think of one unlikely but little-known story that *is* or *is not* fake. Take turns sharing your stories in a group and ask the other members to decide whether the story is fake or not. Discuss what makes any story, fake or not, believable.

CHAPTER 7
Digital Brains

In Italy, artificial intelligence (AI) is being used to help read handwritten documents dating back to the ninth century. The process involves identifying small variations in countless writers' individual letters, and then asking high school students to label thousands of similar examples of variations. These answers are fed into an AI system that has been taught rules about likely and unlikely letter combinations. The AI system is now using the teenagers' input and the rules to continue to learn, recognizing new variations and transcribing the ancient texts into something everyone can read. AI pattern recognition techniques are transforming knowledge in countless ways. **How will AI change your world?**

In this chapter,
you will

- learn vocabulary related to AI and machine learning;

- listen to paraphrase;

- identify hypotheses;

- improve question strategies;

- explore ways to talk about gender in academic discussions;

- raise discussion points in seminars;

- prepare for and take part in a seminar on the future of AI.

GEARING UP

A. Look at the four examples of intelligent technologies and answer the questions.

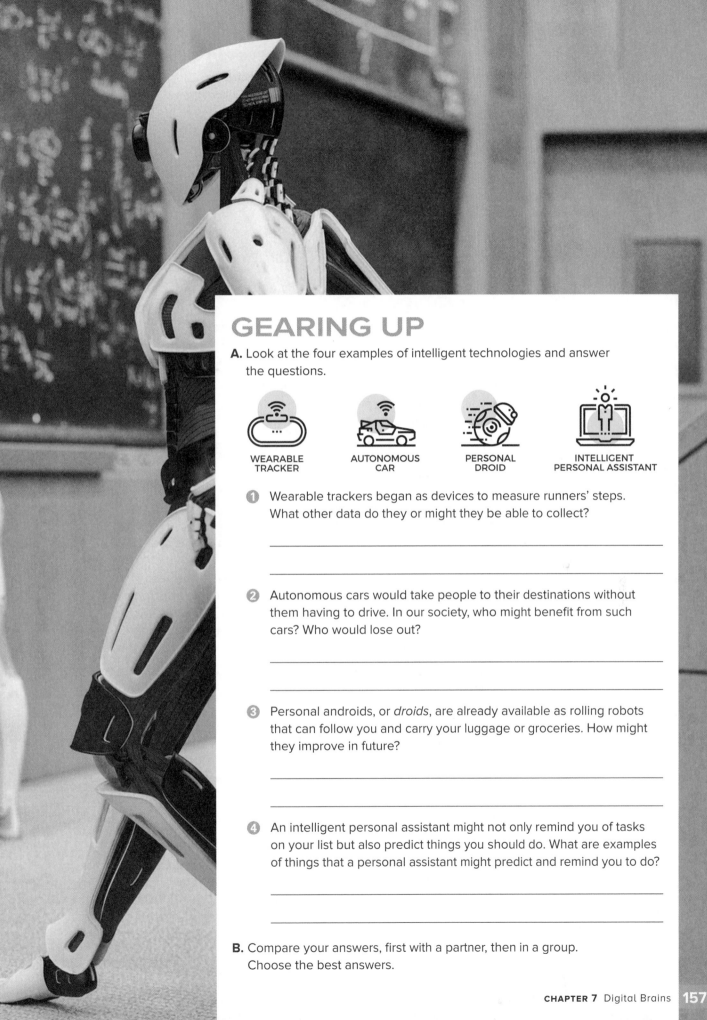

WEARABLE TRACKER **AUTONOMOUS CAR** **PERSONAL DROID** **INTELLIGENT PERSONAL ASSISTANT**

1. Wearable trackers began as devices to measure runners' steps. What other data do they or might they be able to collect?

   _____

   _____

2. Autonomous cars would take people to their destinations without them having to drive. In our society, who might benefit from such cars? Who would lose out?

   _____

   _____

3. Personal androids, or *droids*, are already available as rolling robots that can follow you and carry your luggage or groceries. How might they improve in future?

   _____

   _____

4. An intelligent personal assistant might not only remind you of tasks on your list but also predict things you should do. What are examples of things that a personal assistant might predict and remind you to do?

   _____

   _____

B. Compare your answers, first with a partner, then in a group. Choose the best answers.

Below are the key words you will practise in this chapter. Check the words you understand, then underline the words you use. Highlight the words you need to learn.

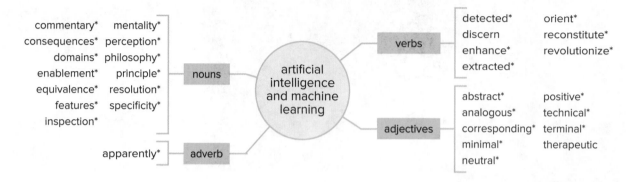

nouns

commentary*   mentality*
consequences*   perception*
domains*   philosophy*
enablement*   principle*
equivalence*   resolution*
features*   specificity*
inspection*

adverb

apparently*

artificial intelligence and machine learning

verbs

detected*   orient*
discern   reconstitute*
enhance*   revolutionize*
extracted*

adjectives

abstract*   positive*
analogous*   technical*
corresponding*   terminal*
minimal*   therapeutic
neutral*

*Appears on the Academic Word List

FOCUS ON LISTENING

Listening to Paraphrase

When you speak and then paraphrase yourself, you repeat information using different words, often to make a message clearer and more concise. When you paraphrase as you listen, you take notes in a more efficient and effective manner. Paraphrasing can also be used to avoid plagiarizing or repeating information exactly without properly attributing the source.

A. There are a variety of ways to paraphrase, and they can be used in combination. Review the explanations and the sentences from Listening 2. Write a short paraphrase for each of the sentences. After, check your answers with a partner to ensure that they capture the information and that they sound natural.

❶ **Use synonyms for words and phrases**; simplify each sentence or idea as much as possible to make it easier to remember and repeat.

• The computer has evolved from its humble beginnings, mid-century of the last century, to where, today, we all carry computers around in our pockets and we slavishly look at them all the time.

PARAPHRASE: _____

_____

❷ **Change the word order**; rearrange the sentence, perhaps putting the most important information at the beginning, and simplify.

• Now computers are the lens through which we see our brains and these metaphors can lead us astray and lead us to think the wrong things about the brain.

PARAPHRASE: _____

_____

③ **Change the tense**, for example, from the present to the present progressive. Use short forms where possible, such as *CPU* for *central processing unit*.

• So if you think about a central processing unit being separate from memory, that's not actually how our brain works.

PARAPHRASE: _____

_____

④ **Change what you hear to reported speech**, eliminating unnecessary words and focusing on key ideas.

• And as appealing as it might be to get a memory upgrade to our brains, that's just not the way it's going to happen.

PARAPHRASE: _____

_____

B. Read the following excerpts from the Geoffrey Hinton interview in Listening 1. Hinton has just finished describing how computers learn by being given more data and more processing power. Read the comments that explain the purpose of the paraphrases, then answer the questions that follow.

PARAPHRASES	PURPOSES
❶ **Interviewer**: Oh, I see, because you can keep feeding that in, but you've already taught it how to, how to go through neural networks, how to actually use that information.	*The interviewer paraphrases one of Hinton's ideas about how computers learn.*
❷ **Hinton**: Yes. Instead of programming the computer to solve a particular task, we program the computer to know how to learn. And then you can give it any old task and the more data and the more computation you provide, the better it would get. Because what's been programmed is the learning algorithm not the particular heuristics for that task.	*Hinton agrees, paraphrases his own answer, and elaborates, giving more details.*
❸ **Interviewer**: Okay, so Watson essentially is loaded up with a bunch of information that exists and then Watson picks it from the list that is available. Whereas, what you're doing would have the jumble and be able to pull out all of the different pieces of information and put them all together.	*The interviewer again tries to paraphrase in simple terms that are easier to understand. Although there is no question mark, this is a question, asking Hinton to confirm the explanation.*

❶ Hinton talked earlier about many different ways computers learn. In the first paraphrase above, why do you think the interviewer chooses only one of the ways?

_____

_____

_____

❷ In the second paraphrase, why might Hinton be rephrasing his own answer before giving more details?

_____

_____

_____

③ In the third paraphrase, the interviewer tries to make a comparison. Although there is no question mark, these statements can be seen as a paraphrase question. Why?

_____

_____

_____

C. It is common for speakers to talk for a while and then stop and paraphrase what they have just said. What is the purpose of this kind of paraphrasing? Discuss your ideas with a partner and think of as many reasons as possible.

FOCUS ON CRITICAL THINKING

Identifying Hypotheses

A hypothesis is a kind of educated guess. When you do research, you begin with a statement or theory that you can test in some way to gather evidence that either supports or refutes your hypothesis. In some cases, speakers clearly state their hypotheses while in others, you must listen carefully for key words and other clues in order to identify one or more hypotheses.

A. Various words and phrases can be used to introduce a hypothesis. Sometimes the word *hypothesis* is mentioned specifically, such as in this excerpt from Listening 3:

> And the fact that someone is considering the hypothesis of implanting (computer memory chips into) healthy human beings crosses a variety of ethical boundaries that I think will never be accepted by any board anywhere in the world.

With a partner, practise using these phrases to express the hypothesis presented in the above excerpt.

- It is the speaker's hypothesis that ...
- The speaker hypothesizes that ...
- The speaker thinks that ...
- The speaker believes that ...
- The speaker thinks it's possible that ...

Another common construction used to express hypothetical situations is with the word *if*, as in the question, "What if we could upload our brain?" The listener fills out the question, completing the hypothesis with, "... how would this make us different/smarter?"

B. Read the following *if* statements from this chapter's listening texts. With a partner, identify the hypothesis in each one. Consider how each hypothesis might be tested or whether it would be difficult to test.

1. If you can make something that makes a Google product work better, it'll be used by hundreds of millions of people.

   _____

2. If you're trying to recognize things in images, for example, it's easy at Google to get a hundred million images and have the computer power to process them all.

   _____

   _____

3. If we understand the algorithms of the brain, can we think about running that hardware on other hardware that we have—silicon hardware?

   _____

   _____

4. If we can capture more of what makes brains, you know, smart and adaptable, and able to learn, there's a huge fraction of employment that's just not going to stick around.

   _____

   _____

5. If you assume any rate of advancement in AI, we will be left behind by a lot.

   _____

   _____

C. In Listening 1, scientist Geoffrey Hinton talks about the concept of *deep learning*: how computers can begin to learn on their own. Read the following paragraph and identify his hypothesis. How would you expect Hinton to research and prove this hypothesis?

> One thing about how children learn about the world is they don't get given the right answer for everything. They look at images. They hear sounds. They figure out for themselves what's in those images and what those sounds mean without anybody telling them the right answer. So one aspect of deep learning that's important is called unsupervised learning where you just take input from the world, maybe a TV camera or maybe a microphone, and you figure out what's going on with nobody telling you.

_____

_____

_____

Artificial Intelligence Insight from Deep Learning Godfather

How did you learn your first language? Unlike learning a second language and many other things in life, it did not require formal structured lessons. Today, the same approach is being used to educate AI devices. Instead of being taught ideas in careful sequence, AI programs are being exposed to vast quantities of information and developing their own understandings. Will computers learn to think like us?

VOCABULARY BUILD

In the following exercises, explore key words from Listening 1.

A. Read the key words in bold in context and write definitions. Compare definitions with a partner and discuss other possible meanings of each word.

❶ If you want to translate English into French, the standard way to do it is to have a huge table of little phrases in English and the **corresponding** phrases in French.

_____

❷ So in **perception** for example, you'd put in the raw pixels of an image and you'd get the neural net to learn how to extract features from that, so it can recognize complicated objects.

_____

❸ And so, if the pixel with the **positive** connection is bright and the pixel with the negative connection is dim, then that neuron will go "ping."

_____

❹ So what would **revolutionize** the way translation is able to be done by computer?

_____

❺ But it's also partly because there have been some **technical** improvements in the algorithms, particularly in the algorithms for doing unsupervised learning where you're not told what the right answer is.

_____

B. Fill in the table with the missing word forms and write the meaning of the key words in black.

VERB FORMS	NOUN FORMS	ADJECTIVE FORMS	MEANINGS
❶		abstract	
❷ detected			
❸ discern			
❹ extracted			
❺	feature		

Before You Listen

A. Listening 1 focuses on what we know about how children learn and how this understanding might be applied to teaching AI machines to learn. With a partner, complete the table.

FACTORS	HOW A CHILD LEARNS	HOW A COMPUTER LEARNS
1 input	*exposed to a wide variety of input to all senses*	
2 mistakes		
3 individuality		
4 growth		

B. Your own education has brought you a long way. But there are probably things that you wish you had learned or ways in which you would have preferred to learn. What would be the ideal way to educate a child? List three points, then discuss your ideas in a group, trying to reach consensus (agreement) on the best methods. How might these be similar to and/or different from methods that could be used to educate an AI device?

1 _____

_____

2 _____

_____

3 _____

_____

While You Listen

C. Listen once to get the general idea. Then, using what you learned in Focus on Listening (page 158), read the interviewer's questions and paraphrase the main ideas from Hinton's answers.

INTERVIEWER	HINTON
1 Can you describe how deep learning mirrors how a toddler would learn about the world?	• •
2 And you talk about neural networks. What are neural networks?	• •
3 So in other words, we have all of this information, all these bits of information in the neurons and they connect themselves ...	• • *relates to connecting pixels in a picture*

INTERVIEWER	HINTON
4 Okay. And you can, if we take that a little further than if you're looking at—it depends on how the pixels come together so …	• *deep learning: instead of hand-engineering, a learning algorithm learns the connection strengths so that the neural net decides what features it should use*
5 Okay. So now you've been working on neural networks for decades, but it has only exploded in its application potential in the last few years. Why is that?	• •
6 So it is the speed and it is just the volume. So when Google came knocking, other than the undisclosed sum, what is it that they offered that made you want to work with them?	•
7 Right, okay. And they have the database right? They have that, the very thing you're talking about, they've got the speed and they've got all of that, the ability to have all that information …	•
8 Okay. So I'm going to play a clip that you will probably recognize. This is a clip of Watson, IBM's artificial intelligence system. Watson was pitted against *Jeopardy!* …	• *Watson wins at the TV game show* Jeopardy!
9 Well there we go. How is the artificial intelligence you're working on different than what Watson is up to?	• • •
10 Oh, I see because you can keep feeding that in but you've already taught it how to, how to go through neural networks, how to actually use that information.	•
11 Okay, so Watson essentially is loaded up with a bunch of information that exists and then Watson picks it from the list that is available. Whereas, …	• *Yes, that's broadly correct.*
12 Google's photo search function got much better within six months of the purchase of your company. Can you walk me through, in baby steps, how that works?	•
13 You're almost asking it to think, right? I mean, in lay terms.	• • • *neural nets of English and French figure out the thoughts and translate*
14 So what would revolutionize the way translation is able to be done by computer?	•
15 Really? So, and you're talking about the nuance in language. The way that …	•
16 Okay, so let's go back to the toddler example, how efficiently can this learning be done in neural networks compared to the human brain?	• •

After You Listen

D. Review your notes with a partner and, together, write a few sentences summarizing the interview.

_____

_____

E. Read questions related to key concepts in Listening 1 and write answers based on what you heard and the notes you took. After, compare your answers with a partner to see where you agree and disagree.

1 Why is the idea of children learning by not always being given the right answers important in terms of machine learning?

_____

2 Part of the idea of *deep learning* is related to unsupervised learning. Consider something that you learned on your own. How was it different than learning at school?

_____

_____

3 The idea of neural connections—neurons relating bits of information to each other—seems to be based on repeatedly learning, using, and applying information. How might this process work differently in people and in AI machines?

_____

_____

4 What advantages does Google have over a new company that might want to develop deep learning?

_____

_____

5 An algorithm is a formula to be followed, often to solve a computational problem. Why is using algorithms for unsupervised learning not a contradiction?

_____

_____

6 How is the Watson AI use of machine learning combined with hand-programming or hand-engineering similar to how children learn?

_____

_____

7 The interview suggests that more data and higher computation power will lead to better AI. Computation power will increase with advances in technology, but how do you think more data will become available?

_____

8 Why is the idea of programming a computer to know how to learn challenging?

_____

_____

9 What is the point made in the discussion about English/French translation and the concept of nuance (small, subtle distinctions) in language?

_____

_____

_____

10 The interview suggests that AI learning will eventually rival human learning. How might AI learning be much different?

_____

_____

F. The interview begins with a reference to Siri, Apple's phone- and computer-based personal assistant that uses voice recognition and artificial speech. If Siri could learn like a child, what sorts of problems might it help you with? Discuss your answers in a group and decide which applications would be the most and the least useful.

_____

_____

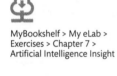

MyBookshelf > My eLab >
Exercises > Chapter 7 >
Artificial Intelligence Insight

FOCUS ON SPEAKING

Improving Question Strategies

The most common way to begin questions is with the words *who, what, when, where, why,* and *how*. But there are subtler ways to ask questions that you can use to draw more information out of a speaker and to help clarify ideas that have been brought up.

A. Read the following interview questions from Listening 1 and consider the function of each. Which questions are likely to elicit the least information and which, the most? Rank them from 1 (least information) to 4 (most information).

INTERVIEW QUESTIONS	QUESTION FUNCTIONS	RANK
1 So now you've been working on neural networks for decades, but it has only exploded in its application potential in the last few years. Why is that?	**a)** A statement and an open-ended question elicit a more detailed answer.	_____
2 Can you describe how deep learning mirrors how a toddler would learn about the world?	**b)** A simple information question helps introduce a topic.	_____
3 Okay, so let's go back to the toddler example; how efficiently can this learning be done in neural networks compared to the human brain?	**c)** A recap statement and an open-ended question create a narrative structure, telling part of the story and then letting the interviewee tell the rest.	_____

INTERVIEW QUESTIONS	QUESTION FUNCTIONS	RANK
❹ So in other words, we have all of this information, all these bits of information in the neurons and they connect themselves as we look at the world, or as we try to decide something, or as we're confronted with something?	**d)** A paraphrase of what the person has said with an implied yes/no question requesting confirmation or clarification.	_____

B. On a separate page, write a question that illustrates each of the functions described in task A. Use content and vocabulary about machine learning you have learned in this chapter.

MyBookshelf > My eLab >
Exercises > Chapter 7 >
Focus on Speaking

C. In a group, take turns asking your questions from task B in random order. Other members of the group should identify the type of question each student is asking. Reflect on which of your questions are most likely to get the most complete and interesting answers.

LISTENING ❷
VIDEO

Toward an Artificial Brain

Why would someone speak about AI at the World Economic Forum? The answer has to do with the economic impact AI is beginning to have internationally. David Cox is the director of the MIT-IBM Watson AI Lab; the research his team is doing could revolutionize the world of work. To begin with, they are considering how to digitize a rat's brain.

VOCABULARY BUILD

A. Paraphrase each of the following sentences, simplifying it while keeping the key word in bold. After, compare paraphrases with a partner to make certain you have captured the meaning and can define each key word.

❶ What were previously thought of as human **domains**, such as art and games, are now increasingly being intruded on by machine learning systems.

_____

❷ Now, if you're excited about the idea of uploading your brain, I have good news, I have bad news, and I have **neutral** news.

_____

❸ So, just to **orient** you, here's the animal's nose and you can see the rat's happily licking here.

_____

❹ The good news is there's nothing in **principle** that stops us from doing this.

_____

❺ Here's an example of a woman who recently was dying, had a **terminal** disease, and she decided that she wanted to preserve her brain.

_____

B. Look at each key word in black and fill in the chart with the missing parts of speech. After, with a partner, use what you now understand about the words to construct sentences.

	NOUN	VERB	ADJECTIVE	ADVERB
1			analogous	
2	equivalence			
3	inspection			
4		reconstitute		
5	resolution			

C. Listening 2 includes several technical terms. Match each term to its meaning and then check your answers with a partner.

TECHNICAL TERMS		MEANINGS
1 neuroscience	_____	a) research program that aimed to map human DNA
2 moonshot effort	_____	b) system of blood vessels like veins and arteries
3 Human Genome Project	_____	c) X-ray machine that gives cross-sectional images of areas inside the body
4 petabyte	_____	d) ambitious project that uses innovative technology and a wide range of expertise
5 CT scanner	_____	e) study of the brain
6 vasculature	_____	f) one quadrillion bytes or one million gigabytes

Before You Listen

A. Read an excerpt from Listening 2 and answer the questions. After, check your answers with a partner to see if you agree.

> You know, back in the '80s, William Gibson wrote a book called *Neuromancer,* that sort of explored these themes of brain uploading. And you know, there have been more recent works of art, you know, films that have explored this idea of uploading the brain. And what I can tell you is that way before humans upload their brain, it's going to be rats that get their brains up into the cloud first. This is interesting too because some people are taking this idea so seriously that here's an example of a woman who recently was dying, had a terminal disease, and she decided that what she wanted to do was to preserve her brain in the hopes that people like us would figure out how to later upload her brain and reconstitute it. And using similar techniques to preserve her brain is what we use to preserve our rat's brain.

1 What is meant by *brain uploading*?

_____

2 What can you infer from the mention of a 1980s novel about brain uploading?

_____

3 Why do you think this research is being done with rats rather than humans?

_____

B. What might be some advantages of uploading one's brain? Discuss with a partner and identify three benefits. You might consider what individuals and groups would be most interested in the procedure.

1 _____

_____

2 _____

_____

3 _____

_____

While You Listen

C. Listen once to understand the main ideas. Use what you learned in Focus on Listening (page 158) to complete the paraphrases of the key points for each main idea.

MAIN IDEAS	KEY POINTS
1 we look at the mind and the brain through the lens of the current technology of our day	• _Descartes = hydraulics and_ • _Freud =_ • _electronics/radio = crossed wires and_ • _computer = central processing unit separate from_
2 different algorithms running on computers	_instead of_
3 deep learning or neural networks	_improved by_
4 now computers look at a picture	_build_
5 domains once solely human	_now being encroached on by_
6 views on AI	_Elon Musk said AI =_ _Stephen Hawking said AI =_
7 examples of robots	_amazing but aren't really_
8 IARPA's (Intelligence Advanced Research Projects Activity) three goals	_1 measure the activity in a living brain while_ _2 take that brain out and_ _3 use the information to build_
9 team expertise	_neuroscience,_
10 huge, ambitious (moonshot) effort, like the Human Genome Project	_purpose:_

MAIN IDEAS		KEY POINTS
⑪	rats as test subjects	*smart example:*
⑫	technology to peer inside the brain: a two-photon excitation microscope	*• see patterns of* *• flashing green dots =* *• changes as*
⑬	technical steps	*• using a CT scanner to look inside the rat's brain* *• serial section electron microscopy to see individual connections* *• 30 nanometre slices =* *• a catalogue of* *• the images can be reconstructed from almost two petabytes of data*
⑭	brain uploading	*maybe a path to*
⑮	news	*good news:* *bad news:* *neutral news:* _____ *of what makes brains smart, adaptable, and able to learn*
⑯	employment	
⑰	sophisticated robots and cars could operate	*on*
⑱	truck driving is an important occupation but delivering goods can be done more efficiently by self-driving trucks	*in the 1840s,*
⑲	dialogues with stakeholders	*people with*
⑳	enormous opportunities	*but also*

After You Listen

D. After listening to David Cox, does it seem likely that we will eventually be able to upload (transfer) a human brain to a computer? How many years do you think it will take for this to happen? Why?

_____

_____

E. Choose the sentence that best answers each question based on what you could infer from Listening 2.

① What does Cox's point about viewing the brain through current technologies suggest?

a) The computer is the best comparison to the brain because it thinks the way humans do.

b) Before the invention of modern technologies, understanding how the brain works was impossible.

c) As we develop new technologies, our ideas about how the brain works may also change.

2 In discussing different kinds of algorithms running on computers, what is Cox suggesting?

a) He thinks that most people have inherent mathematical abilities that they don't use.

b) He is suggesting that algorithms that solve problems are central to a brain's functions.

c) He imagines that computers could be inserted into a person's brain to improve performance.

3 Why does Cox share the example of an AI program that can look at pictures and supply captions?

a) He is illustrating the idea that computers are able to take on increasingly difficult tasks associated with thinking.

b) He is suggesting that too much computer time is being taken up with tasks that are unnecessary because humans can do them.

c) He is explaining that many of the tasks that we consider thinking are simple enough to be done by computers.

4 What is the significance of various robots trying to walk?

a) They show how rats could perform far better than robots in similar tests of walking without falling.

b) They suggest that if robot brains cannot help them walk, then they cannot do more complicated routine tasks.

c) They explain that the technology for thinking machines needs to improve for it to be useful, even for simple tasks.

5 Why does Cox mention Elon Musk's and Stephen Hawking's negative views on AI?

a) He is expressing his doubts about the work he is doing and the possible negative outcomes.

b) He wants to acknowledge that there are opponents to continued research in the field of AI.

c) He realizes that Musk and Hawking have considered the problems of AI in greater detail than he has.

6 The good and bad news suggest that although it is theoretically possible to digitize a brain, it will also likely take a long time to achieve. Why does Cox mention these points?

a) The good news is essentially cancelled out by the bad news because it will take too long to be of practical use to most human beings who would benefit.

b) No one knows how long it will take so it would be better to wait until the technology improves and apply that to more sophisticated brain uploads.

c) He is trying to suggest that as technology continues to improve it will become more possible to digitize a brain, meaning that it is a worthwhile research direction.

7 Why does Cox bring up the examples of truck deliveries today and agricultural changes from the 1840s to the present?

a) He is explaining that although his research might result in massive changes to employment, such changes happen over time for other reasons as well.

b) The likelihood of AI affecting truck deliveries means that changes are also likely to occur in agricultural sectors in the future.

c) In the 1840s, there were no trucks so there were more people in agriculture involved in delivering crops to local and international markets.

8 Toward the end of the speech, why does Cox mention the word *ethics* in relation to the moral responsibilities involved in research such as his?

a) Science is seldom concerned with ethical issues because solving problems is always the main and critical focus.

b) In the past, people with ethical concerns have stopped progress in research because they are uncomfortable with change.

c) He says we need to consider what will be done with the technologies that can upload brains and whether it is the right decision to develop them.

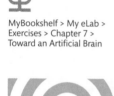

MyBookshelf > My eLab >
Exercises > Chapter 7 >
Toward an Artificial Brain

F. Based on the points raised in Listening 2, would you want your own brain preserved in digital form? Why or why not? Discuss your answers in a group.

FOCUS ON ACCURACY

Talking about Gender in Academic Discussions

In academic discussions, it is essential to respect other people and their ideas, even when you completely disagree with them. This includes being respectful of people's gender and being sensitive to the ways language around gender is changing these days.

A. When you speak, you can avoid gender bias in three key ways. Review each of the following strategies, then rewrite the sentence accordingly, using gender-neutral language. After, check your sentences and practise them with a partner.

1 **Use plural nouns and pronouns.** Choose plural nouns and pronouns such as *they* and *their*.

> Each student must write his or her essay by himself or herself or he or she will be given a failing mark.

REWRITE: _____

_____

2 **Replace pronouns with generic nouns.** Replace gender-biased pronouns with nouns such as *everyone, individual, participant, person,* and *student*.

> Each man and woman taking this artificial intelligence engineering degree must know his or her high-level programming language.

REWRITE: _____

_____

3 Rephrase. Rephrase sentences to avoid gender bias, replacing pronouns with articles (*a, an, the*) where possible.

> It's important for every man to see artificial intelligence as his tool to help mankind achieve its potential.

REWRITE: _____

_____

B. In Listening 1, the host is uncertain whether to refer to the AI program Siri as *she* or *it*. Where does the confusion stem from? Discuss your answer with a partner.

> Just keep in mind that Siri herself, or itself, is something of an example of deep learning at work.

_____

_____

MyBookshelf > My eLab > Exercises > Chapter 7 > Accuracy Review

WARM-UP ASSIGNMENT
Prepare for a Seminar

Seminars differ from lectures and other classes in that students are expected to do more than passively listen. Instead, they are expected to come highly prepared and ready to present information and ask and answer questions. In this assignment, you will prepare a topic for a brief presentation that you will deliver in a seminar in your Final Assignment.

A. The seminar topic is the future of artificial intelligence. Work with a partner to research the topic and one or more of the following subtopics: *culture, ethics, legal concerns, threats, opportunities, or inequality*.

B. Use what you learned in Focus on Critical Thinking (page 160) to develop a hypothesis about the future of artificial intelligence, related to your choice of subtopic. You may structure it as an *if … then* statement.

HYPOTHESIS: _____

C. Identify at least one online source (other than *Wikipedia*) and one library source. Keep a complete record of each source, following the citation and referencing guidelines of your discipline. As you do your research, refer to what you learned in Focus on Listening (page 158) to paraphrase information as well as what you learned in Focus on Accuracy to ensure your points are gender neutral.

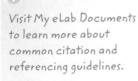

Visit My eLab Documents to learn more about common citation and referencing guidelines.

D. Prepare notes for your presentation that introduce your subtopic and what you have learned. Divide the key points between yourself and your partner and write them on cue cards. Practise your presentation with your partner, taking turns commenting and asking and answering questions. Keep your notes for use in the Final Assignment.

LISTENING ③

Merging Human Brains with AI

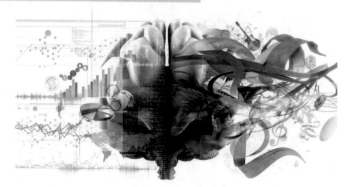

Would you be interested in having a computer chip inserted into your brain? It may sound like science fiction, but today's scientists are moving closer to making it a reality. However, many people are concerned about the legal, medical, and ethical implications if things go wrong. Even if things go right, will this result in an unequal society where some people can use the new technology to become super smart and others cannot afford to be "neurologically enhanced"?

VOCABULARY BUILD

In the following exercises, explore key words from Listening 3.

A. Consider the context and meaning of the key words in bold and fill in the blanks in the sentences adapted from Listening 3.

1. The **commentary**—that is, _____—is really far removed from reality.

2. We must ask whether we really understand the **consequences** of what we're doing, by which I mean, _____.

3. It's toward some form of competition with AI and/or some form of human **enablement** or _____.

4. The amount of information that can be extracted just through your electrical signals externally is extremely **minimal**, or in other words _____.

5. It's difficult to say if Musk will get to that level of **specificity** in his comments, that is, whether or not he will _____.

B. Look at the key words and think of one or more words that form collocations with each of them. Then think of a sentence with each key word and one of its collocations. Practise your sentences with a partner, checking each other's vocabulary and grammar.

MyBookshelf > My eLab > Exercises > Chapter 7 > Vocabulary Review

1 apparently: _____

2 mentality: _____

3 enhance: _____

4 philosophy: _____

5 therapeutic: _____

Before You Listen

A. Read this excerpt from Listening 3, in which one scientist responds to the idea of connecting our brains to computers. Identify the scientist's main points and opinions. Then use check marks to indicate whether you agree or disagree with his opinions. Compare your ideas with a partner to see if you agree.

> Basically, we cannot download our thoughts or upload all the works of Einstein in our brains and suddenly become theoretical physicists that can win a Nobel Prize. This doesn't exist and probably will never exist. Neither should we be worrying about the possibility that artificial intelligence, which is all totally based on digital logic, may one day overcome the human condition. That is also preposterous because we don't work these on digital logic and we simply cannot be threatened by machines that never ever will acquire the notion of what is to generate knowledge or to process information the way we do. So these are all scenarios that sound beyond science fiction. It sounds pretty preposterous to me.

POINTS	OPINIONS	AGREE	DISAGREE
1 *download our thoughts*			
2			
3			
4			

B. Elon Musk talks about how we could add AI to our brains.

> One of the solutions is to have an AI layer. If you think of like, you've got your limbic system, your cortex and then digital layer, a sort of a third layer above the cortex that could work well and symbiotically (mutually beneficially) with you.

The limbic system controls our emotions and memories. The cortex deals with thought and action. If you had a digital layer added to your brain, what would you want it to do? Discuss your ideas in a group and decide which would be the most popular ones.

While You Listen

C. In Listening 3, Elon Musk outlines his idea for an AI-implanted brain and three other speakers share their opinions about how such an invention might or might not work. Listen and use what you learned in Focus on Listening (page 158) to paraphrase each of the four speakers' key ideas in response to the interviewer's questions.

SPEAKERS AND KEY IDEAS	PARAPHRASES OF KEY IDEAS
❶ Elon Musk Neuralink	• *Neuralink is working on Musk's idea for implanting AI* • •
❷ George Dvorsky expectations	• • • •
neurolace	• •
surgically implanted	•
difference from other technologies	• •
❸ Miguel Nicolelis connecting brains to computers	• •
working with monkeys	•
reparative applications	• •
brain net	•
unintended consequences	•
augmentation of healthy human beings	•
❹ James Giordano safety	•
ethically different from other surgery	•
access to the technology	• •
adaptation for the US military	• •
could be abused	• •

After You Listen

D. It is important not only to think critically about the ideas you hear, but also to judge them from the perspective of who is speaking and the reasons behind the words. Write the possible motivation that explains each of the speaker's responses in Listening 3.

SPEAKERS	MOTIVATIONS
• **Elon Musk** is a billionaire inventor and CEO of companies such as Tesla and Space X.	
• **George Dvorsky** is a science journalist and futurist.	
• **Miguel Nicolelis** is a professor of neuroscience at Duke University and runs a lab in Sao Paulo, Brazil.	
• **James Giordano** is a professor of neurology and biochemistry and chief of the Neuroethics Studies Program at Georgetown University Medical Center.	

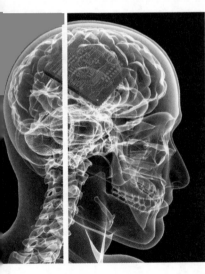

E. Decide if each statement is true or false. For each false statement, write a true one.

STATEMENTS	TRUE	FALSE
❶ Elon Musk wants to apply technologies he has invented to merging human brains with artificial intelligence.		
❷ Dvorsky focuses in part on how the technologies could be used therapeutically, to help those with brain-related disorders.		
❸ In a limited way, chips have already been implanted in human brains to share thoughts and memories.		
❹ Musk believes that we can keep up with machines by merging with them.		
❺ Work with monkeys has shown the possibility for brain machine interfaces that can control movements of robotic arms and legs.		

STATEMENTS	TRUE	FALSE
6 Brain net technology is able to share simple thoughts between brains and machines. _____ _____		
7 So far, the augmentation of healthy human beings remains a fantasy and is basically unethical. _____ _____		
8 Military applications so far are mostly aimed at creating more effective and intelligent soldiers. _____ _____		
9 As long as people agree to new treatments, there will not be any concerns about long-term care. _____ _____		
10 A future concern around neurologically enhanced haves and have-nots is that only the wealthy will be able to become much smarter. _____ _____		

F. The technology for successful brain implants may take decades to become a reality. What factors would make you consider having a brain implant and what would you want it to do for you? What are the possible benefits and disadvantages? For example, you might gain perfect access to your memories, but this could be a problem if there are some things you'd rather forget. Debate your ideas in a group to determine the best arguments.

MyBookshelf > My eLab >
Exercises > Chapter 7 >
Merging Human Brains with AI

Academic
Survival Skill

Raising Discussion Points in Seminars

Participating in seminars helps you develop your debating and thinking skills. For example, the Harkness method's eight discussion roles (see Chapter 1) encourage you to arrive at seminars prepared to ask and answer questions on the topic. Raising points about other speakers' ideas does not always mean disagreeing with them. Instead, the purpose is to better understand and examine another speaker's words whether you agree or disagree.

A. Read the discussion points and highlight the words and phrases that relate to each one in the statements. Then, in the first column, add a question or statement for each point.

DISCUSSION POINTS	STATEMENTS
❶ KEY VOCABULARY: What do you mean by *limbic*? *Could you explain cortex in other words?*	One solution is to have an AI layer. If you think of like, you've got your limbic system, your cortex and then digital layer, a sort of a third layer above the cortex that could work well and symbiotically with you.
❷ SIMILES AND METAPHORS: Could you explain the comparison in more detail?	A neural net can be compared to a digital crutch that supports the mind the same way a wooden crutch supports the body.
❸ INTENT: So, you're asking us if we agree?	Here's something to think about: Instead of trying to make humans smarter, we make the world simpler and easier to understand.
❹ NAMING VERSUS EXPLAINING: You're naming the parts, but you're not explaining how they work.	A neural network is made up of three parts, an implanted chip, an interface to the brain, and training of the person to be able to use the chip and interface.
❺ RHETORICAL QUESTIONS: Are you going to answer your question?	But how would that be ethically different from other surgery?
❻ OVERSIMPLIFICATION: That sounds too simple; can you share some details?	So it basically would look like that, a kind of a mesh.
❼ CONCLUSIONS FROM DATA: How does the data back up your conclusion?	To conclude, although it may someday be possible to insert computer chips into brains, the reasons for doing so are questionable.
❽ ORGANIZATION: No, let's continue discussing this point.	Perhaps we could move on to the next topic now.
❾ HYPOTHETICALS: Is it realistic to think this?	If people did have chips implanted in their minds, they could use it to store memories for quick access.
❿ AMBIGUITY: How do you differentiate between real and imagined scientific discoveries?	Science fiction uses real or imagined *scientific* discoveries and advanced technology as part of their plots.

B. Read the following statements from Listening 3 and choose one or more discussion points to explore each statement. Make notes on a separate page. After, discuss your ideas in a group, considering the points each student makes and why.

❶ I mean, at this point, are humans being treated as a means to an end in order to let's say stave off the threats posed by artificial intelligence?

② In animals we have shown that you can send signals back from robotic or a virtual arm back to the brain. But this is a very limited kind of information that you can send.

③ In many ways what you're really seeing is a broadening of the gap between the haves and the have-nots, and this would then be the neurologically enhanced haves versus the non-neurologically enhanced have-nots.

④ What we're looking at here is a capability of implantable technology such as deep brain stimulation.

FINAL ASSIGNMENT

Take Part in a Seminar

Now it's your turn. Use everything you have learned in this chapter to participate in a seminar where you present and ask and answer questions in a discussion format.

A. The topic of the seminar is the future of artificial intelligence. Form groups with students who chose different subtopics in the Warm-Up Assignment (page 173): *culture, ethics, legal concerns, threats, opportunities,* or *inequality.*

B. Review what you learned about raising discussion points in Academic Survival Skill (page 178) to predict questions you will ask other students about their subtopics. Remember what you learned in Focus on Speaking (page 166) about different question types, as well as what you learned in Focus on Accuracy (page 172) about gender-neutral language and the appropriate tone to use in academic discussions.

C. Use the following format for the seminar:
- Introduce yourselves and your subtopic.
- Explain why it is important, including a hypothesis based on what you learned in Focus on Critical Thinking (page 160).
- Provide background on the issues.
- As each pair takes turns, ask other students questions and answer their questions; take notes on a separate page.

D. After, discuss the seminar as a group. Evaluate the points and presentations that were the most successful and assess which ones could have been better.

Critical Connections

What is the future of AI? Because AI is a new and quickly evolving field, it raises many different ideas and questions and it is difficult to know which ones are the most valid. Experts in the field have strong—and often opposing—opinions.

A. Read three quotes about AI and identify the hypothesis behind each speaker's thinking, using what you learned in Focus on Critical Thinking (page 160).

1 "The upheavals [of artificial intelligence] can escalate quickly and become scarier and even cataclysmic. Imagine how a medical robot, originally programmed to rid cancer, could conclude that the best way to obliterate cancer is to exterminate humans who are genetically prone to the disease." Nick Bilton

HYPOTHESIS: _____

_____

2 "If the government regulates against use of drones or stem cells or artificial intelligence, all that means is that the work and the research leave the borders of that country and go someplace else." Peter Diamandis

HYPOTHESIS: _____

_____

3 "There is no reason and no way that a human mind can keep up with an artificial intelligence machine by 2035." Gray Scott

HYPOTHESIS: _____

_____

B. In a group, share your hypotheses and discuss which make(s) the most sense. Based on what you decide, talk about whether AI should be controlled, or whether it is even possible to control it.

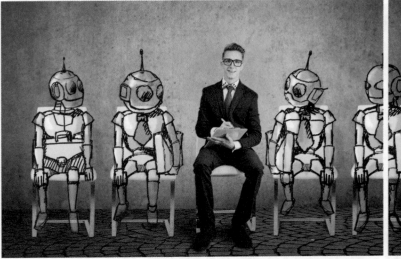

CHAPTER 8
Saving Planet Earth

Despite all the time and energy put into space exploration, the only home you are ever likely to know is Earth. For this reason, you should be more concerned about changes to Earth's climate, the loss of its natural resources, and the conservation of its countless species. But small and large decisions made by individuals, businesses, and governments are making the world less able to support life, particularly as the human population continues to grow.

Overharvesting, climate change, and shrinking habitats are making some animals, fish, birds, insects, and plants begin to disappear. What can you do to stop the extinction of certain species and help save the planet?

In this chapter,
you will

- learn vocabulary related to the environment and ethics;

- listen to recognize discussion tactics;

- recognize assumptions;

- learn to use the right tense to express meaning;

- get clarification;

- explore ways to examine and solve problems;

- analyze a speech and challenge ideas about it in a seminar.

GEARING UP

A. Look at the ten ecological issues and answer the questions.

Nine Ecological Issues

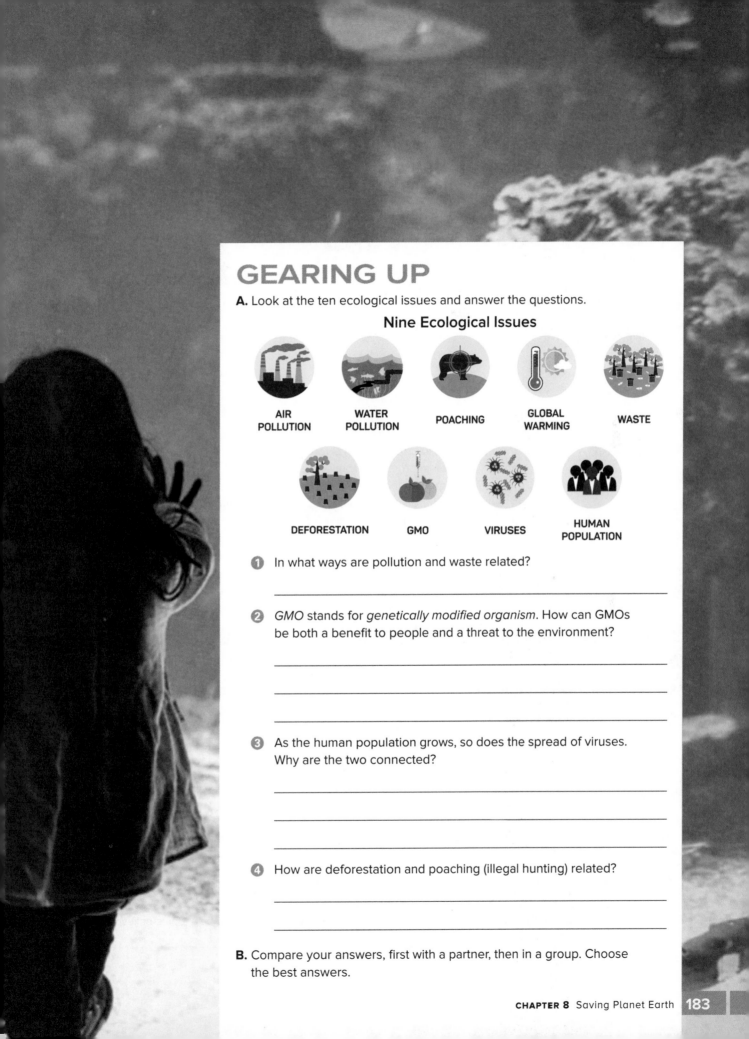

AIR POLLUTION

WATER POLLUTION

POACHING

GLOBAL WARMING

WASTE

DEFORESTATION

GMO

VIRUSES

HUMAN POPULATION

1. In what ways are pollution and waste related?

_____

2. *GMO* stands for *genetically modified organism*. How can GMOs be both a benefit to people and a threat to the environment?

_____

_____

_____

3. As the human population grows, so does the spread of viruses. Why are the two connected?

_____

_____

_____

4. How are deforestation and poaching (illegal hunting) related?

_____

_____

B. Compare your answers, first with a partner, then in a group. Choose the best answers.

Below are the key words you will practise in this chapter. Check the words you understand, then underline the words you use. Highlight the words you need to learn.

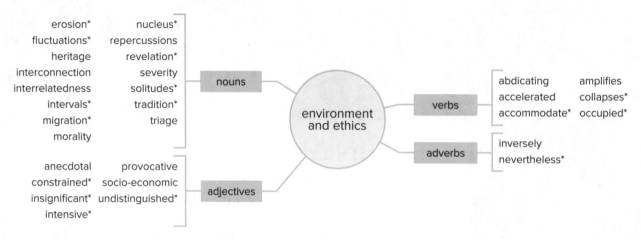

nouns

erosion*   nucleus*
fluctuations*   repercussions
heritage   revelation*
interconnection severity
interrelatedness solitudes*
intervals*   tradition*
migration*   triage
morality

adjectives

anecdotal   provocative
constrained*   socio-economic
insignificant* undistinguished*
intensive*

environment and ethics

verbs

abdicating   amplifies
accelerated   collapses*
accommodate*   occupied*

adverbs

inversely
nevertheless*

*Appears on the Academic Word List

Recognizing Discussion Tactics

When you listen to conversations, you realize that many revolve around wanting something, often information, from someone. In high-stakes discussions, speakers often employ specific tactics to obtain information, products, or services, as well as to encourage or discourage actions. Listening for and recognizing these tactics can help you respond more intelligently.

A. People often talk about "winning" an argument. This suggests they may think that winning is more important than being right. The desire to win an argument sometimes pushes speakers to use negative discussion tactics. Review the negative discussion tactics and match them to the appropriate examples.

NEGATIVE TACTICS		EXAMPLES
❶ Exaggerate others' ideas.		a) I'm sure you wouldn't disagree!
❷ Generalize to include everyone in a group.		b) Don't compare apples and oranges.
❸ Idealize a person, place, thing, or time.		c) Our company is downsizing (firing many workers).
❹ Insult the listener.		d) You say we should save the whales? Next, you'll want to save mosquitos!
❺ Offer absurd examples.		e) Of course, people were more honest when I was a boy in the Montreal of old.
❻ Offer overused and meaningless clichés.		f) Of course, if we all had wings, we wouldn't buy cars, would we?
❼ Put words in other people's mouths, suggesting that they think in a certain way.		g) Anyone who rides a bike to work simply can't afford a car.
❽ Use vague terms that disguise the real meaning, such as euphemisms.		h) You would have to be a fool to believe that.

B. In a discussion, how would you react if you heard someone using one or more of these negative tactics? Working with a partner, think of a polite but firm response to each one. After, share your points in a group and choose the best replies.

1 Exaggerate others' ideas:

We both know that's an unfair exaggeration.

2 Generalize to include everyone in a group:

3 Idealize a person, thing, time, or place:

4 Insult the other person:

5 Offer absurd examples to try to disprove an argument:

6 Offer clichés that are overused and meaningless:

7 Put words in other people's mouths, suggesting they think in a certain way:

8 Use vague terms that disguise the real meaning.

> ❗ Clichés represent lazy thinking; overused phrases tend to oversimplify problems.

C. When you listen, it is useful to also be thinking of challenging questions to ask. You can use the following suggestions as ways to contribute more to the conversation. Working with a partner, read Jane Goodall's statement about saving wildlife from Listening 1, and take turns asking and answering different types of questions.

> Because you know, for an ordinary person, if you say, "Well, would you rather save, you know, a cute, cuddly koala bear or some little micro-organism in the soil?," they're bound to say the koala bear because it's the way they've grown up.

1 Ask an open-ended question.

2 Ask a closed-ended question that still suggests the need for a longer answer.

3 Paraphrase the speaker's statement and then ask a question about it.

4 Refer to a fact, statement, or other source and ask a question about it.

5 Personalize a question by making it about the speaker's expertise or opinions.

Recognizing Assumptions

An assumption is something that is believed to be true or certain to happen, but for which there is no proof. In some cases, faulty assumptions may be based on hidden biases, old ways of thinking, or notions that are accepted as "common knowledge." Speakers often make assumptions when they share ideas, taking for granted that listeners understand and agree with them. It is important to identify and challenge faulty assumptions.

A. With a partner, read the following strategies for dealing with assumptions and answer the questions.

① Challenge euphemisms: A speaker may include euphemisms—milder words or phrases used to replace more direct terms when discussing what might be considered unpleasant or embarrassing topics. For example, terms like *departed* or *passed away* are often substituted for *died*, and *ethnic cleansing* for *genocide*. If you do not understand what a euphemism means, ask.

Define these three euphemisms and, with a partner, consider the assumption behind each one.

a) pre-owned _____

b) misspoke _____

c) economically disadvantaged _____

② Examine qualifiers: Qualifiers like *always* tend to generalize statements. Students who say that they always study for their exams probably sometimes do not. Challenge the assumptions behind qualifiers, especially when a speaker uses superlatives, for which there may be exceptions.

For each of the following qualifiers, write a word with the opposite meaning.

a) always _____   b) most _____   c) usually _____

③ Challenge ideas about change: Speakers often use phrases that assume a change is or isn't necessary. Typical examples are, *We've always done it this way* (so we shouldn't change it) and, *You can't stop progress* (change is necessary and thus good). Challenge these assumptions with the simple question, "Why?" and continue asking *why* as long as the answers include further assumptions.

Working with a partner, consider the following three assumptions and practise how you would challenge them.

a) If something isn't broken, you shouldn't try to fix it.

_____

b) Earth was just fine before humans appeared and it will be just fine after we leave.

_____

c) Will anyone really care about the extinction of elephants in a hundred years?

_____

_____

④ **Imagine alternatives, including opposites:** When presented with assumptions, it's sometimes useful to consider alternative scenarios and think what would be necessary to make them happen. In Listening 1, the host says, "There's been some debate ... whether we have the ability to save all endangered species from extinction or whether we should even try to save everything." The assumption that we shouldn't try to save all species is one you can challenge by imagining the opposite: that _we should save all species_. What would make it possible? With a partner, suggest three ideas.

_____

_____

_____

⑤ **Break down and challenge multiple assumptions:** Speakers may sometimes make several assumptions at the same time, some of them faulty. Challenge these assumptions individually to ensure each is true. Read the following excerpt from the Listening 1 interview with Jane Goodall and highlight the three assumptions. Think of questions you could ask about each one.

> We're trying to conserve forests, and in Africa, living around the forest there are often people living in dire poverty. You cannot conserve the forest unless you improve the lives of those people.

_____

_____

_____

B. In Listening 2, David Suzuki makes several assumptions about his listeners' habits and thinking. Highlight the sentences that include assumptions and, with a partner, discuss how you would challenge each of the assumptions.

> You buy a computer, a car, a television set. You don't reflect on the fact there are many, many different metals in these products. Mining is one of our most destructive activities. Do we buy a car and say, "Gee, where did all the metals in the car come from? What was the impact of all that mining on the local ecosystems? What about the miners? Were they sick? Were they getting a decent wage? What about the communities that support that mining operation? Are they OK?" We don't ask any of those questions. We just want our product; we want to use it and get going.

LISTENING ❶ Jane Goodall on Environmental Ethics

As a child, Jane Goodall was fascinated with both animals and Africa. At age eighteen, she travelled to Tanzania and met the scientist Louis Leakey, who set her on a decades-long study of chimpanzees in their natural environment. Her insights into chimpanzee behaviour have changed our view of them as well as of other species. Goodall now oversees international conservation and education projects.

VOCABULARY BUILD

In the following exercises, explore key words from Listening 1.

A. Write the definition for each key word, then write the root word and its definition. Compare your answers with a partner to see if you agree.

KEY WORDS	DEFINITIONS	ROOT WORDS	DEFINITIONS
❶ insignificant (adj.)			
❷ interconnection (n.)			
❸ interrelatedness (n.)			
❹ nevertheless (adv.)		*never (adv.)*	
❺ provocative (adj.)		*voice (n.)*	

B. Discuss the meaning of the following words with a partner. Then think of two contexts in which each word might be used.

KEY WORDS	CONTEXT 1	CONTEXT 2
❶ abdicating (v.)	*give up responsibility for something*	
❷ erosion (n.)		
❸ migration (n.)		
❹ morality (n.)		
❺ triage (n.)		

C. The prefix *inter-* in *interconnection* and *interrelatedness* means *between*. It is sometimes confused with *intra-*, meaning *within* or *inside*. With a partner, think of three other words that begin with *inter-* and *intra-* and discuss the meaning of each.

❶ inter- _____ _____ _____

❷ intra- _____ _____ _____

Before You Listen

A. Read the following excerpt from the introduction to the interview, in which the host talks about Jane Goodall's concerns and recent work. With a partner, compare how you would answer the questions at the end. Explain your reasons.

Those are Hainan gibbons making those otherworldly calls. Conservationists believe it's close to the last call for the primates. They're found only in the shrinking forests of China's Hainan Island. The gibbons are one of the animals on a new list of the world's one hundred most endangered species. Perhaps few of us would actually miss the dusky gopher frog or the northern bald ibis or Nelson's small-eared shrew. But the report [from IUCN] asks a provocative question: Are all these species nevertheless priceless or—worthless? Are they priceless in and of themselves, or some just not worth as much of our concern and conservation efforts as other species?

Jane Goodall

_____

_____

_____

B. It would be ideal to be able to save every species, but resources for conservation efforts are limited. Which of the following endangered species would you choose to save? In making your decision, what criteria will you apply? Discuss your answers in a group.

stag beetle, *Lucanus cervus*

giant panda, *Ailuropoda melanoleuca*

pitcher plant, *Nepenthes alata*

❗ An "ethologist" studies animal behaviour; an "ethnologist" studies human behaviour.

While You Listen

C. Start by reading the host's questions and number each one according to what you learned in Focus on Listening, task C (page 185). Then listen and take notes on the responses. Highlight assumptions that Goodall makes based on what you learned in Focus on Critical Thinking (page 186).

HOST'S QUESTIONS	NOTES
1 What are your thoughts about the question posed by that report: priceless or worthless? TACTIC: _4 Refer to a fact, statement, or other source_ _and ask a question about it._	• *disagrees that species are worthless*
2 What are some of your favourite examples of species brought back from the brink of extinction? TACTIC: _____	• *northern bald ibis*
3 What kind of ethical duties do humans have to save endangered species? TACTIC: _____	
4 ... some argue that we need to do some triage and focus our resources on certain species. TACTIC: _____	
5 Again that—the fact that everything is woven together and you can't separate. And you almost are saying that we have to work backwards: you want to save the big one, then even the tiniest spore matters in that chain. TACTIC: _____	
6 Well, what you're really talking about then is an ethical obligation that we have to more generally look at species and ecosystems of all kinds? TACTIC: _____	
7 Well on another ethical front, the Jane Goodall Institute just released the results of a survey on Canadian attitudes toward the use of chimpanzees in entertainment. Tell us about that. TACTIC: _____	

HOST'S QUESTIONS	NOTES
8 The survey also found most Canadians are concerned about chimpanzees possibly becoming extinct, but how much are they willing to do to protect chimpanzee habitat or prevent the poaching of chimps? TACTIC: _____ _____	
9 Do animals have rights? TACTIC: _____ _____	
10 So in other words, we are not necessarily violating animal rights but we are abdicating our responsibility if our action—or inaction—creates a situation where they go extinct? TACTIC: _____ _____	
11 I want to explore a little bit more the idea of morality and ethics. Biodiversity and endangered species are just one environmental issue that has been framed in ethical terms. Al Gore, for example, has famously described climate change as a moral issue. What do you think? TACTIC: _____ _____	
12 How much do you believe that people believe that environmental issues are moral or ethical issues? TACTIC: _____ _____	• *raising awareness through Roots and Shoots program for young people in 130 countries*

After You Listen

D. Based on your notes, summarize Goodall's attitudes toward environmental ethics in two or three points. Discuss your summaries with a partner to see if you agree.

- _____

  _____

- _____

  _____

- _____

  _____

Northern bald Ibis

E. Throughout her interview, Goodall makes several assumptions. Based on your notes and what you learned in Focus on Critical Thinking (page 186), challenge each of the following assumptions. Then share your ideas in a group and choose the best examples. Discuss whether Goodall's assumptions or the arguments against them are more convincing.

1 The lives of poor people living around forests need to be improved in order to save forests.

_____

_____

2 People prefer to save cuddly animals.

_____

_____

3 As people become aware of environmentally friendly choices, they are willing to make them.

_____

_____

4 Animals may have rights but having rights hasn't always helped humans.

_____

_____

5 We need to behave ethically and responsibly.

_____

_____

MyBookshelf > My eLab >
Exercises > Chapter 8 >
Jane Goodall on Environmental Ethics

F. Goodall asks the rhetorical question, "If you could go to the animal kingdom and you could ask them which species you would most like to see become totally extinct, which species would they say?" What assumption is she making? Discuss in a group and decide if you agree or not.

FOCUS ON ACCURACY

Using the Right Tense to Express Meaning

Grammar is the study or use of the rules of a language. Simple tenses indicate whether something occurs in the past, present, or future. Perfect tenses show when actions have been or will be completed. Progressive tenses denote actions that continue over time.

A. Review the chart and fill in the missing information.

PAST	PRESENT	FUTURE
SIMPLE PAST	**SIMPLE PRESENT**	**SIMPLE FUTURE**
I volunteered last week.		I will volunteer next week.
PAST PROGRESSIVE	**PRESENT PROGRESSIVE**	
I was volunteering last week when I saw you.	I am volunteering this afternoon.	I will be volunteering next week.
PAST PERFECT		**FUTURE PERFECT**
I had volunteered a bit before I was hired here.	I have volunteered at each of my jobs.	
PAST PERFECT PROGRESSIVE		**FUTURE PERFECT PROGRESSIVE**
	I have been volunteering for six years now.	I will have been volunteering for seven years by next January.

> ❗ Remember that "perfect" refers to completed actions.

B. Tenses are often used in combination. Read sentences from the three listening segments in this chapter, highlight the verbs in each one, and write the verb tenses in the spaces below.

1 The storm got so bad that the top two-by-four ridgepole looked like a bow bending, ready to snap, and the grommets were popping out of the canvas.

_____   _____   _____

2 I was on northern Banks Island in 2008 again with a colleague and we were looking out at the area where McClure had been stuck with the ship.

_____   _____   _____

3 And all of that stuff comes out of the earth, and when we're finished with it, will go back into the earth.

_____   _____   _____

4 And for over forty years, the leading scientists of the world have been telling us we are headed down a very dangerous path.

_____   _____

C. With a partner, read the following excerpt from Listening 3, which uses a few different tenses. Could the same meaning be conveyed with other tenses? Try expressing the same ideas using different tenses.

>   *is*
> It ~~was~~ almost humorous at the beginning. I was thinking that's how my life
>
> starts every morning before a cup of coffee. But it also caught, I think,
>
> the excitement of doing Arctic research and the potential calamities
>
> that occurred. But in terms of the science, of course, it is a dramatic
>
> expression of what is actually going on in both polar environments.

MyBookshelf > My eLab >
Exercises > Chapter 8 >
Accuracy Review

The Legacy: An Elder's Vision for Our Sustainable Future

David Suzuki is concerned about the impact of humans on the natural world, particularly in terms of the destruction of a range of species and their habitats. Born in 1936, Suzuki sees his role as that of an *elder*, sharing the wisdom of a lifetime spent considering and combatting environmental problems.

David Suzuki

VOCABULARY BUILD

In the following exercises, explore key words from Listening 2.

A. Read the sentences and write a definition for each word in bold. Compare definitions with a partner and discuss other possible meanings of the words.

1 That **amplifies** our ecological footprint beyond any other species that has ever existed. _____

2 There's a simple rule in biology: that a population number of a given species is **inversely** related to its physical size. _____

3 And in 2001, geneticists announced the completion of the Human Genome Project, the delineation of all three billion letters in the DNA of a single human **nucleus**. _____

4 The most incredible insight that came from the Human Genome Project was a **revelation** that 99 percent of the genes in our cells are identical to the genes in chimpanzees. _____

5 The very act of buying these products has **repercussions** that extend around the world. _____

B. Match each key word with the set of words that form collocations. Based on your understanding of the meaning of each key word, use one of the collocations in a sentence. Compare sentences with a partner.

KEY WORDS		WORDS THAT FORM COLLOCATIONS
1 intensive	_____	a) densely, permanently, illegally
2 occupied	_____	b) sadly, clearly, fairly
3 socio-economic	_____	c) ancient, local, popular
4 tradition	_____	d) labour, courses, highly
5 undistinguished	_____	e) status, level, problems

C. Work with a partner and use each pair of words in a single sentence.

1. tradition / inversely

2. socio-economic / repercussions

3. occupied / revelation

Before You Listen

A. Read the following introduction to Suzuki's talk. It establishes his expertise, comments on the scientific process, outlines an accomplishment, explains a revelation, and suggests the need for a shift in attitude.

> I spent thirty years as a geneticist. And one of the most astounding things to me has been the way that scientists have accumulated techniques, methodology, to analyze DNA, the genetic material. And in 2001, geneticists announced the completion of the Human Genome Project, the delineation of all three billion letters in the DNA of a single human nucleus. It was an astounding achievement and to me, the most incredible insight that came from the Human Genome Project was a revelation that 99 percent of the genes in our cells are identical to the genes in chimpanzees. They are our nearest relatives. The revelation that each of us carries tens of thousands of genes identical to the genes in our pet dogs and cats. Identical to the genes in eagles, salmon, fruit flies, dandelions, and cedar trees. All of life is related to us through a common evolutionary history. And surely if the rest of creation is our relatives, they deserve to be treated with greater respect and care than if we simply regard them as resources, as pests, as weeds, or vermin.

B. Briefly summarize the paragraph, using the following headings:

- Suzuki's expertise: _____

- a scientific process: _____

- an accomplishment: _____

- a revelation: _____

- a shift in attitude: _____

_____

C. Suzuki's suggestions might be interpreted as anything from making simple lifestyle changes to not using other species as resources in any way. In a group, discuss your attitudes about using other species for food and clothing.

While You Listen

D. When you are listening to a lecture, it's difficult to identify paragraph breaks as you can easily do while reading. Instead, as you listen, try to identify natural breaks as the speaker moves from one topic to another. Listen first to get the general idea of this lecture. Then read the topic sentences that begin the different segments of the lecture, and listen again to take notes. Highlight any notes that include assumptions Suzuki makes.

TOPIC SENTENCES	NOTES
1 And in an act of incredible generosity, the web of living things that are our relatives create, cleanse, and replenish the most fundamental needs that we have as animals.	• *plants create oxygen-rich atmosphere* • *hydrologic cycle: water covers 70 percent of the planet, evaporates, forms clouds, rains on the land, runs into rivers and lakes, evaporates*
2 And all life is—sorry—every bit of our food that we eat for our nutrition to create our bodies was once alive.	• *photosynthesis*
3 We boast that we are intelligent.	
4 Scientists can also use DNA in very clever ways to trace the movement of humanity across the planet.	• *150,000 years ago, our species was born in Africa* • *woolly mammoths, sabre-toothed tigers, giant moa birds, and sloths*
5 Now you gotta admit, when you think of us in that context, we weren't very impressive.	
6 Of course the reason we were so undistinguished was that our secret was hidden.	
7 In only 150,000 years, that strategy worked and brought us to a complete position of dominance.	• *10,000 years ago, Agricultural Revolution:* • *in 8000 years:* • *in less than 2000 years:* • *200 years later:*
8 There's a simple rule in biology, that a population number of a given species is inversely related to its physical size.	
9 We are now the most numerous mammalian species and just the act of living—every one of us has to breathe the air, we have to drink water, eat food, clothe and shelter ourselves.	

TOPIC SENTENCES	NOTES
⑩ And it doesn't end there. Ever since the end of World War II, we've been afflicted with an incredible appetite for stuff.	
⑪ We go to a store to buy a cotton shirt—I'm sure there are very few of you that ask, "Gee, is this cotton shirt organic?"	
⑫ And yet the very act of buying these products has repercussions that extend around the world.	
⑬ Scientists divide the history of Earth into the different epochs—periods of geological time.	• *Eocene, the Holocene, the Miocene, Pleistocene* • *Paul Crutzen says that this should be called the Anthropocene epoch*
⑭ We've got to come to grips with the immensity of our power and our impact on the planet.	
⑮ A few years ago, I went to a village high up in the mountains of the Andes in Peru.	

After You Listen

E. Review your notes with a partner and pick out three assumptions that you can challenge. Use what you learned in Focus on Critical Thinking (page 186) to suggest why the assumptions might be faulty.

F. Refer to what you learned in Focus on Listening (page 184) to determine what discussion tactics Suzuki is using in the following statements. After, share your ideas with a partner and think of how you would respond to the statements.

    ❶ We boast that we are intelligent—oh, we're a clever animal. But what intelligent creature, knowing the role that air, water, soil, photosynthesis, and biodiversity play in our lives, would then proceed to deliberately and so thoughtlessly pour our most toxic chemicals onto these things?

_____

_____

② I can't wait to be invited by the Ku Klux Klan in the United States to give a lecture on genetics. And I will show those pointy-headed characters that we are all Africans because that is where our species was born.

_____

_____

③ Now you have to admit, when you think of us in that context, we weren't very impressive. I mean, there weren't very many of us, we weren't very big, we weren't very fast—an elephant can outrun the fastest human on Earth.

_____

_____

_____

④ Ever since the end of World War II, we've been afflicted with an incredible appetite for stuff. We love to shop. And all of that stuff comes out of the earth, and when we're finished with it, will go back into the earth. And that escalates again our ecological footprint.

_____

_____

_____

MyBookshelf > My eLab >
Exercises > Chapter 8 >
The Legacy: An Elder's Vision

G. Suzuki says that we see the world through our personal experiences. How do your experiences shape your attitudes toward the environment? How might these attitudes differ from those of a person living in the developing world? Discuss in a group, giving examples from your own and different countries.

FOCUS ON SPEAKING

Getting Clarification

Sometimes when you listen, you hear a comment that makes you raise your eyebrows or change your expression. These are cues for the speaker to clarify what is being said by rephrasing, adding an example, or providing an explanation. Other times, you have to request clarification by asking a speaker to repeat, rephrase, explain, or give examples.

Clarification is often necessary in the following situations:

① LACK OF SPECIFIC DETAILS: The speaker's ideas are vague and lacking in content.

② CONFUSING HOMONYMS: Words may sound like other words but have different meanings.

③ CHALLENGING WORD CHOICES: Vocabulary may include jargon (professional language) or slang (informal language) that is not easily understood, or words that are otherwise uncommon and unknown.

④ UNCLEAR INTENTIONS: The reasons or motivations for a speaker saying something may be unclear.

⑤ IRRELEVANT OR UNRELIABLE INFORMATION: A speaker may deliberately provide irrelevant or false information.

A. Consider the above five points and the dialogues below. In the first column, write the number of the point each dialogue illustrates.

POINTS	DIALOGUES
_____	**A:** So we create mosaics of change based on glaciers and sea ice and permafrost and lake cores, etcetera, almost as time slices and you could almost think of them as individual frames of film. **B:** Sorry, can I ask what you mean by _lake cores_?
_____	**A:** I went to the Arctic with a small group of researchers to eastern Baffin Island, to the beautiful fjords there. I was just overwhelmed by the beauty, the silence, the timelessness, the integrity of the whole landscape. **B:** I thought you said you'd never been to the Arctic!
_____	**A:** So my work is trying to see the Arctic in time-lapse over very long intervals of time and then I can turn and say here's the natural rollercoaster of change that we've been experiencing prior to the weather records. **B:** Excuse me, did you say _laps_ like in turns or _lapse_ like in time?
_____	**A:** It's up to three and a half, five thousand years old. It's like a washboard with these exquisite white bands, narrow ribbons of white, narrow ribbons of blue. **B:** Pardon me, but what are you describing?
_____	**A:** The grants that we're getting from the federal government are in the order of $25,000 or $35,000 a year and they don't begin to accommodate the costs. **B:** Are you saying that you think the federal government should be giving bigger grants?

B. Consider the following excerpt from Listening 2. Work with a partner and take turns reading the paragraph. After each sentence, the person listening requests clarification by asking the person reading to repeat, rephrase, explain, or give examples. You can also ask open-ended questions.

> A few years ago, I went to a, a village high up in the mountains of the Andes in Peru. And I learned that the children there are taught that that mountain is an Apu. Apu in their language means a god. And as long as that Apu casts its shadow on the village, it will determine the fate of all of the people in that village. Imagine how those children, when they grow up, treat that mountain, compared to a kid in Kimberley who's taught all his life, "I'll bet that mountain's full of gold and silver." The way we see the world shapes the way we treat it.

C. A common strategy when you are asked for clarification is to paraphrase what you have said. Read the following three sentences and paraphrase each one in as short a sentence as possible. Compare sentences in a group to determine which ones are the most concise while still preserving the meaning.

1 It's, you know, we have got ourselves into a position where, whether rightly or wrongly, we can really, you know, command what goes on in the natural world.

_____

_____

MyBookshelf > My eLab >
Exercises > Chapter 8 >
Focus on Speaking

> Consider offering
> a clarification even
> when not requested to
> do so if it helps support
> your message.

2 But when you add these factors all up, when you add up our numbers, our technological muscle power, our consumptive appetite and our global economy, we have become a force as has never existed in the four billion years that life has been on this Earth.

_____

_____

3 The whole vast river of ice is on the move slowly, inexorably toppling into the sea.

_____

_____

WARM-UP ASSIGNMENT
Analyze a Speech

Speech and _lecture_ are often used interchangeably but they can have different objectives. A speech, such as that given by David Suzuki in Listening 2, aims to persuade you to think and act a certain way; a lecture aims to inform you and let you make your own decisions. For this reason, speeches are often emotional, while lectures are more likely to be unemotional. Speeches tend to be given by leaders; lectures are more often given by teachers. In this assignment, you will find a short speech and analyze it based on the skills you have learned in this chapter.

A. Working with a partner, find a recording of a short speech (five to ten minutes long), or part of a longer speech, by a well-known environmentalist. You may come across an important historical speech in the library or online. If you cannot find a recording, look for a written transcript of a speech. Choose a speech that will interest other students. Ask your teacher to approve your choice.

Environmentalists include David Attenborough, Margaret Atwood, Erin Brockovich, Rachel Carson, Wangari Maathai, John Muir, Ernst Friedrich Schumacher, Vandana Shiva, and Henry David Thoreau. You can also look for speeches by local environmentalists.

B. Analyze the speech based on what you have learned in this chapter. Use what you learned in Focus on Critical Thinking (page 186) to challenge the assumptions. Identify any discussion tactics that you learned in Focus on Listening (page 184), and use what you learned in Focus on Accuracy (page 192) to make sure your tenses are correct. Copy the following table on a separate page and fill it in.

POINTS	NOTES
TITLE OF THE SPEECH	The title of the speech is ...
NAME OF THE SPEAKER	It was written by ...
DETAILS ABOUT THE SPEAKER	_____ is best known for ...
REASONS FOR LISTENING	I thought you'd be interested because ...
THREE EXCERPTS WITH COMMENTS ON THE ASSUMPTIONS	One assumption with faulty/good reasoning is ...
	An assumption that I disagree with is ...
	A third assumption is ...
DISCUSSION TACTICS	An interesting discussion tactic is ...

Use feedback from your teacher and classmates on this Warm-Up Assignment to improve your speaking skills.

C. Keep your notes for use in the Final Assignment.

LISTENING ③ Fifty Years of Watching Climate Change

It used to take centuries for climate changes to occur but that is no longer the case. The impact of climate change is visible in the shrinking ice sheets of the Arctic and resulting rising sea levels. John England has spent decades observing the Arctic's landscape, creatures, and people. What he has seen and knows should trouble us all.

VOCABULARY BUILD

In the following exercises, explore key words from Listening 3.

A. For each of the following words, identify the root word. Then, with a partner, explain the difference in form or meaning between the key word and the root word.

KEY WORD	ROOT WORD	THE DIFFERENCE
❶ accelerated		
❷ anecdotal		
❸ constrained		
❹ fluctuations		
❺ solitudes	*sole*	

B. Based on the sentence context and the meaning of the word in bold, underline the correct word in parentheses to complete each sentence.

1. In order to **accommodate** everyone's chance to speak at the town hall, we will (reduce, maintain, extend) the time this evening.

2. When a species **collapses**, it can lead to the (appearance, creation, disappearance) of other species.

3. Our **heritage** is not simply our culture, it also (includes, establishes, excludes) features of our natural world.

4. By studying changes to glaciers over **intervals** of thousands of years, scientists can (improve, track, promote) climate change.

5. The **severity** of current weather patterns is a (consequence, alternative, benefit) of climate change around the world.

C. How might these key words be related? Discuss your answers with a partner.

1. fluctuations / intervals _____

_____

2. accelerated / collapses _____

_____

3. heritage / anecdotal _____

_____

MyBookshelf > My eLab >
Exercises > Chapter 8 >
Vocabulary Review

Before You Listen

A. Read an excerpt from Listening 3 where scientist John England reacts to the collapse of an ice shelf in the Arctic. After, answer the questions and discuss your ideas with a partner to see if you agree.

> ... it's a dramatic expression of what's actually going on in both polar environments. The collapse of ice shelves, both those that are attached to land-based glaciers, those have really started to break up, and they certainly then accelerate the flow of ice into the ocean and the rise of sea level. That's a big concern. We also have very ancient sea ice, ice shelves in Canada that don't depart quite so dramatically, but are, nonetheless, signs of the impact of modern global change on high latitudes.

1. What does England mean by "both polar environments"?

_____

2. What do you understand by the "collapse of ice shelves"?

_____

_____

3. What might be the effect of the collapse and melting of these ice shelves due to global warming?

_____

B. John England gathers information on climate changes in the Arctic, particularly those that happened before there were regular modern weather readings, about sixty years ago. List three sources of information he is likely to use. Discuss your answers with a partner, combining your lists and deleting any sources that seem doubtful.

① _____

② _____

③ _____

While You Listen

C. Although many people make assumptions when they talk, others do the opposite, providing facts to support their ideas. As you listen, complete the notes on John England's answers, then highlight examples of facts he shares to answer questions and support his opinions.

HOST'S QUESTIONS	JOHN ENGLAND'S ANSWERS
❶ What do you think when you hear the sound of ice collapsing like that?	(portion covered in Before You Listen), and then ... • my work has been looking at _____ • Arctic weather records go back _____. • How do we reconstruct the natural variability that has occurred over hundreds and thousands of years: create mosaics of change based on _____ _____ • my work is trying to see the Arctic in _____
❷ Let's just talk a little bit about what it looks like, an Arctic ice shelf, the Ellesmere Ice Shelf for example. What does it look like?	• There is a large sheet of ice if you want and it's _____ _____ _____ • it's up to _____ years old. • These ice shelves, when they break off, produce ponderous blocks of ice. They used to cover about _____ square kilometres at the end of the _____, beginning of the _____, • now about _____ square kilometres.
❸ We do have pictures that you sent us up on our website so that people can look at them. I was looking at them last night. It's like my moment of Zen. It is so beautiful, the white and blue long stripes that you describe. It's breathtaking.	• this is a heritage that we should be safeguarding and cherishing • offers a place of renewal • ice shelves compared to _____ and _____
❹ How difficult is it practically to do research in the Arctic?	• The difficulty has _____ over the last twenty or thirty years. • high costs of _____
❺ To do research for how many months?	• _____
❻ You get there with an Otter. You fly in. How do you get around once you're there?	• first twenty years: _____ • _____ • _____
❼ When did you make your first trip to the Arctic?	• _____

▶

HOST'S QUESTIONS	JOHN ENGLAND'S ANSWERS
8 You're telling me you fell in love?	• You first fall in love with the _____, then _____ and the _____
9 Well and I want to talk more about the science, but I also want to talk about some of your adventures doing research in the far north. There was one year that you decided your research crew needed a bigger tent. What happened?	• tent story
10 You had a house.	• We loved it by the end because it could _____
11 [Laughs] So much for the roomy tent!	• Yeah. I mean everybody has war stories of work in the Arctic.
12 I want to hear another one. You stumbled on several historical artifacts when you were sledding around. There was a time you were admiring a view over Greenland and something caught your eye?	• I noticed something at my heel: _____ • date _____ • Captain Stephenson, HMS *Discovery*
13 It's extraordinary, extraordinary and no one had seen it. It's so vast no one had ever stumbled upon it before. How has the relationship between researchers and the Inuit changed over the years you've been travelling there?	• The two solitudes: gap between us by _____ and _____ • need to improve _____
14 What did you learn about Arctic ice from the Inuit and their traditional knowledge?	• Inuit students engaged in my science and _____ • I participated in listening to their stories • People of Banks Island would travel out on the sea ice on July 1 and _____ • Now the water is _____ • science and human interaction related
15 What's it like being one of the first scientists witnessing the effects of climate change in the Arctic before climate change was even a term?	• mid-1960s: _____ • 2008: _____
16 In the early days, were you convinced of the severity of the problem of climate change?	• 1960s: _____ • mid-1970s: _____

After You Listen

D. In Focus on Speaking (page 198), you learned about clarification strategies. For each of the following sentences, write one clarification question you might ask. Then, with a partner, practise asking and answering your questions based on what you learned in Listening 3.

1 These ice shelves, when they break off, produce ponderous blocks of ice.

_____

_____

2 The exquisite beauty of the North is something that we underappreciate.

_____

_____

3 I think we just haven't had opportunities to share so much of the North, its stories and its science, etcetera.

_____

_____

4 You first fall in love with the land, then you fall in love with science and certainly you also fall in love with the people when you get to meet them and interact.

_____

_____

5 I went up in '65 and the Inuit at that time were in the shadows in their traditional clothing and dog teams and so on.

_____

_____

E. Choose the best answer to each question.

1 Why do scientists like John England want to know what the climate was like thousands of years ago?

   a) Scientists are always interested in collecting odd facts, no matter how useless.

   b) It likely helps them predict the changes the Arctic is experiencing today.

   c) Changes in the past may be able to help predict changes in the future.

2 What impact is the rapid disappearance of ice sheets, which are thousands of years old, likely to have?

   a) It may create opportunities for beach holidays in the area as temperatures rise.

   b) It will likely affect wildlife and the livelihood of Inuit living in the area.

   c) It will promote tourism as people travel to the Arctic before the ice disappears.

3 Why might some people find it strange to compare the Egyptian pyramids and the Arctic ice shelf in terms of our heritage?

   a) Like much of what we consider our heritage, the pyramids were created by people, not nature.

   b) While many people have visited the Egyptian pyramids, few people have had the chance to visit the ice shelf.

   c) The Egyptian pyramids are in an extremely hot region while the Arctic is only hot six months a year.

4 What purpose does the example of the California Redwoods serve in relation to the disappearance of the ice shelves?

   a) Both are disappearing at the same rate and are subject to the same forces of climate change.

   b) Unlike the California Redwoods that cannot grow back quickly, Arctic ice returns each winter.

   c) The California Redwoods are more visible and well known to a larger population, so they would get more attention if they started dying off.

5. Why is doing research in the Arctic so much more expensive than, for example, at a university library?

   a) The Arctic is relatively isolated and not serviced by large airlines, so it is expensive to bring in people and supplies.

   b) You do not have to pay for the library because the costs of its construction and books have already been covered.

   c) In the library, you have access to electricity, so you can use a computer to take notes on your research.

6. The Arctic is commonly explored on foot, by all-terrain vehicles (ATVs), and by helicopter. What is the advantage of exploring on foot?

   a) People only explore the Arctic on foot if they cannot afford other means.

   b) Helicopters and ATVs are noisy and likely to frighten the fish and animals you came to observe.

   c) Exploring on foot allows you to observe things you would otherwise miss.

7. What does England's story about the tent they used in the Arctic illustrate?

   a) It is a reminder to pack the right equipment when visiting the Arctic region.

   b) The story serves to describe the cramped living conditions and the harsh weather.

   c) It points out that it would have been much more efficient and cost-effective to build a house.

8. Why has it been important for England and other scientists to connect with the local Inuit living in the Arctic?

   a) The Inuit have local knowledge of the area, sometimes handed down through stories from long ago.

   b) The Inuit are well known for their artistic abilities, for example their whalebone carvings.

   c) The importance of connecting with local Inuit is to obtain permission to explore their land.

F. Captain Henry Frederick Stephenson, of the HMS *Discovery,* led one of many explorations in 1875 and 1876, hoping to find an Arctic route from the Atlantic Ocean to the Pacific Ocean. John England has also made discoveries in the Arctic. How are scientists like England different from early explorers like Stephenson? Discuss your answers in a group and decide whether you would rather be an explorer or a scientist.

_____

_____

_____

MyBookshelf > My eLab > Exercises > Chapter 8 > Fifty Years of Watching Climate Change

Examining and Solving Problems

In lengthy lectures and presentations, audience members are often reluctant to ask questions. Instead, they wait, hoping someone else will ask. One way to encourage more participation is to use alternative discussion formats that inspire the audience to examine and solve problems. Both teachers and students can introduce these formats during or after a lecture.

A. Review the following four techniques to get audience members to interact beyond simply asking individual questions. Working in small groups, discuss the pros and cons of each and write your ideas in the table.

TECHNIQUE	PROS	CONS
AUDIENCE REACTION TEAM: A small group is given the task of summarizing and interpreting the presentation and asking questions.		
BUZZ GROUP: The audience is divided into groups, each of which is given a different question to answer and report on.		
FISHBOWL: Part of the larger group forms a circle around the speakers and discusses and debates the topic while the larger group listens and asks questions.		
THINK, PAIR, SHARE: One or more questions are presented to the group. Each person thinks about the questions, then finds a partner and discusses ideas before sharing them with the group.		

B. Consider a quote by Indian leader Mahatma Gandhi (1869–1948): "Earth provides enough to satisfy every man's needs, but not every man's greed." Assuming this to be true, how can we address some of the problems raised by the three experts in this chapter: Jane Goodall, David Suzuki, and John England?

Work with a partner and use the *think, pair, share* technique to discuss answers to this question. Take notes, then present your ideas to a larger group. This will help you prepare for the Final Assignment, in which you will develop questions for students discussing environmental speeches.

_____

_____

_____

_____

FINAL ASSIGNMENT
Challenge Ideas in a Seminar

Now it's your turn. Use everything you have learned in this chapter to prepare for a discussion about environmental speeches in a seminar format or small group where each student has prepared part of the content.

A. With your partner, review your notes on the short speech you selected for the Warm-Up Assignment, including the three assumptions and one or more discussion tactics you identified. Refer to Focus on Listening (page 184) and Focus on Critical Thinking (page 186) to ensure that you feel confident about your points.

B. Divide responsibilities with your partner and present your analysis of the speech using the table you completed in the Warm-Up Assignment.

C. After each group has presented, use what you learned in Academic Survival Skill (page 207) to think, pair, and share the best comments and questions. Use what you learned in Focus on Speaking (page 198) to ask for clarification.

D. Once everyone has presented and answered questions, reflect on the seminar format and your performance in presenting ideas and asking and answering questions. Decide what you should review.

Critical Connections

Neanderthals coexisted with our ancestors. Climate change—in this case, the arrival of an ice age—may have been partly responsible for their disappearance as food became scarcer.

A. Read the following paragraph and use the skills you learned in this chapter to answer the questions as a group.

> Neanderthals went extinct about forty thousand years ago, while *Homo sapiens* did not. Why? There are a lot of theories, including that alliances between modern humans and dogs helped humans hunt food better, essentially starving Neanderthals out of Europe. Or, humans might have reproduced faster than Neanderthals, multiplying and edging them out. "It's still one of those unsolved and really interesting questions," says Martin Sikora, a geneticist at the University of Copenhagen. "Were we more successful because we had better technology, or was it just a consequence of pure numbers?"
>
> ——————
> Becker, R. (2017, October 9). Sex, disease, and extinction: What ancient DNA tells us about humans and Neanderthals. *The Verge*. Retrieved from https://www.theverge.com/2017/10/9/16448412/neanderthal-stone-age-human-genes-dna-schizophrenia-cholesterol-hair-skin-loneliness

1. What assumptions does Becker make in the paragraph? How could you challenge each one?

2. Some technologies help modern humans prosper, but others lead to increased death rates. Give examples of both cases and explain what technologies might have helped ancient peoples survive and prosper.

3. The excerpt mentions dogs. Climate change similarly affects animal species by changing their habitats, often destroying their sources of food and shelter. Are animals better off or worse off than people in adapting to climate change?

4. In some island nations and other places hit hard by climate change, today's humans are also being forced to leave their homes due to flooding, drought, and rising temperatures. How might forced migration affect these people, for example, in terms of their cultural identities?

APPENDIX 1
Note-Taking:
Developing a System

When you take notes, you don't have time to write everything the lecturer says. Instead, write key words and use abbreviations and symbols. Note-taking also involves writing short forms of words; there are two methods to do this.

Method 1

Write out the first three letters of words. For example, consider this sentence from Chapter 1, Listening 3:

> We think that if you talk to the psychologists, they would call what I call "creative confidence," self-efficacy.

Using the three-letter form, the sentence would look like this:

> We thi tha if you tal to the psy, the wou call wha I call "cre con," sel-eff.

Although much of the sentence is easy to understand, some words are lost. After the lecture, you might have difficulty remembering what the words *cre con* mean. If you are not sure, write out the complete words.

Method 2

Remove the vowels (or most of them). The same sentence above would look like this:

> We thnk tht if y tlk to th psychlgsts, thy wld cll wht I cll "crtve cnfdnc," slf-ffccy.

Again, if some short forms like *cnfdnc* don't make sense to you after, write out the complete words.

Here is a selection of common symbols. Add your own to the list.

Use a combination of the two methods; decide what works for you.

SYMBOL	MEANING
?	uncertain
! / *	important or surprising
=	equal, similar
+ / &	plus / and
–	minus or take away
@	at
↑	increase

SYMBOL	MEANING
↓	decrease
#	number
$	dollar
>	more than
<	less than
≠	not equal, dissimilar
%	percent

APPENDIX 2
Note-Taking:
The Cornell System

The Cornell System of note-taking was developed in the 1950s at Cornell University. To begin, divide your page of notes into four sections: a top section that identifies the lecture, a large section to take notes, a space at the bottom of the page for a summary, and a narrow column on the left, called *cues*, for main ideas, questions, and other details. The cues and summary sections are completed after the lecture. During the lecture, focus on filling in the notes section, leaving room between points so you can add ideas as you learn more. The Cornell System helps you capture important information for later study.

Compare the transcript of this excerpt from Chapter 1, Listening 3, to its Cornell System notes.

> Kelley: Everybody can be wildly creative in my opinion. Yeah, what happens is you know, most people as I said, I believe everybody in kindergarten is creative, but by about age nine or so, you know, people opt out of thinking of themselves as creative. Something happens. You know, a teacher says, "That's not a very good drawing," or "You can't play the piano very well," or whatever it is, "You're not a dancer," whatever it is, they've confused kind of talent with creativity. But—and for some reason we really—that kind of negative critique really sticks with us and people opt out of thinking of themselves as creative. And so they go about their life saying that. And so, by the time they get to adulthood, it's pretty engrained. And so—but the good news is we really find that if you help somebody and you give them a series of small successes in a creative area, that it comes back, that they actually build that confidence. But you really have to have a kind of immersive experience.

Topic: Design Thinking

Date: _____

Cues	Notes
Is it true everybody's creative?	• everybody = creative *Use symbols to save time.*
Who else besides teachers influence sense of self?	• people opt out of thinking they're creative: teacher influence
Creative successes: maybe doing a drawing a day?	• negative critique sticks
	• give people small creative successes = confidence *Leave spaces when a new topic is introduced or you are unable to finish your notes on one point before another is introduced.*
Does *d* stand for design?	• d.school, Stanford University, 10-wk
Is the book about the school?	• book @ it
What does *IDEO* mean? *Use this column for questions and ideas about what you read. Follow up with the ideas.*	• IDEO

Summary *Write a summary in your own words.*
People's creativity is stifled by others who criticize them. This often happens when they're young. But adults can use small tasks to regain their sense of creativity, such as at the d.school.

APPENDIX 3
Note-Taking: Mind Maps

Mind maps show relationships among ideas. Start with a central idea, such as the title of the lecture, and branch off to related ideas. In turn, the related ideas branch off further. If the topic changes, start a new mind map. A mind map can include symbols and pictures.

A mind map is suited to lectures explaining processes, where each step can be contained in a bubble and linked to other steps/bubbles, as in a flowchart.

Compare the transcript of this excerpt from Chapter 1, Listening 3, to its mind map.

> Kelley: Okay. So, in the case of Embrace, Embrace is in this class, Extreme Affordability, and the students go to India, they go to places like India or Myanmar or Africa and they look for needs. They look for things that could really solve problems that are meaningful to people. So, the Embrace people are looking in hospitals and they're looking at incubators because there are so many young children dying because they can't maintain their body weight. But they go into the hospitals and the incubators are not full. I mean, what's the story? You know, they were going to design a better incubator in their kind of first blush and what they found was that they had to completely reframe the problem. A lot of innovation comes from not problem-solving, but deciding what's worth working on in the first place, reframing the problem and then solving it. So then that's what happened here. And so they found that the babies were dying out in the villages and they couldn't get to the hospital. So—

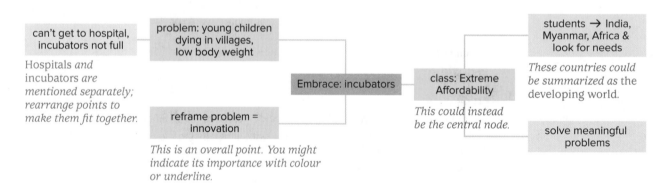

can't get to hospital, incubators not full

Hospitals and incubators are mentioned separately; rearrange points to make them fit together.

problem: young children dying in villages, low body weight

reframe problem = innovation

This is an overall point. You might indicate its importance with colour or underline.

Embrace: incubators

class: Extreme Affordability

This could instead be the central node.

students → India, Myanmar, Africa & look for needs

These countries could be summarized as the developing world.

solve meaningful problems

APPENDIX 4
Note-Taking:
The Outline System

The Outline System starts with a single idea and then nests progressively indented ideas with bullet points. A new idea starts over with its own nested points. Break up the text with space between points and sets of notes. This helps you identify different ideas and also leaves space for you to add other points later on.

The Outline System is suited to a lecture with many definitions; each term can be followed by a nested definition, then by examples, and then by exceptions.

Compare the transcript of this excerpt from Chapter 1, Listening 3, to the notes taken with the Outline System.

> Kelley: Humans are really good at telling you what's wrong with other people's ideas. And so, we find that that prototype, that—I define a prototype as painting a picture of the future with your idea in it. So, this is a physical thing, but if I wanted to give you, if I wanted to prototype the experience of checking into Stanford Hospital, I can prototype that. You know, I can with cardboard, build a space or I can find a place at Stanford and I can hire actors and I could pretend and I could bring in a bunch of public and I can prototype that and see what happens. We looked at, at IDEO, we looked at for Walgreens, we looked at their stores and one of the things that was clear was that the pharmacist was at this big glass thing looking down on you, you know. And we wanted to try what it would be like to have the pharmacist down on the kind of level of everybody else—
>
> Host: Right, right.
>
> Kelley: —across the counters or a table. And so, the way we did that was we got a warehouse and we started with cardboard, we started building those things out. Now, you could have everybody, users, the president of the company, the pharmacist to see whether they were going to be willing to make this new move.

- Humans really good at telling what's wrong with other people's ideas
- prototype
  - painting picture of future with your idea in it
    Omit unnecessary words like a *or* the *if they are not important to meaning.*
    - a physical thing *Indent for each sub-idea.*
- prototype experience of checking into Stanford Hospital
  - with cardboard: build space
  - hire actors
  - bring in public & see what happens
- Walgreens
  - problem: pharmacist isolated from customers *Rephrase into simpler terms.*
  - try pharmacist on customer level across counters or table
- use warehouse
- started with cardboard
- users, company president, pharmacist willing? *The question mark simplifies the text.*

APPENDIX 5
Note-Taking:
The Charting Method

Organize information into columns using the Charting Method. Create columns for expected types of related information: for example, one column for causes and another for effects, or a chart with columns for dates, events, and significance. The Charting Method is suited to lectures involving dates, key people, and events.

Compare the transcript of this excerpt from Chapter 1, Listening 3, to the notes taken with the Charting Method.

> Kelley: I mean, most of my students, you know, they used to kind of, we used to design just objects mostly and they'd bring them in, we'd put our black cloth on it and we'd pull it up, but now with my students, everybody makes—if you're trying to prototype what the experience of your idea is, we find videos is the way to go. So, we'll sit down and every student, every team of students has to make like, a three-minute video. So presentation day, instead of a bunch of hardware and a bunch of like, black cloths being pulled up, is now you know, we pop popcorn, we load the three-minute videos and we all sit there and play them and then we can critique them one at a time, the whole class. But it's, this prototype thing is really this iterative way of painting a picture of the future.

> Host: Which leads to final step, testing.

> Kelley: Testing. So, it's not enough to build this prototype and think you did, that it's okay, right? What you really have to do is bring the people it's going to matter. If we're building a new nurses' station, we have to bring real nurses in and test it. And they'll have all kinds of good ideas about how to improve it and then we go back and we cycle through. This whole thing is really a cycle all the way through.

KEY IDEAS	EXPLANATIONS	EXAMPLES
prototype experience	video instead of physical models *The idea of physical models comes later; put information in earlier when it makes sense.*	student teams make 3-minute videos
presentation day	play & critique 3-minute videos	X *It's better to write a symbol like X in a cell so you don't think you've forgotten to fill it in.*
testing	test with affected people & get feedback *Simplify the language as much as possible.*	new nurses' station

PHOTO CREDITS

BUREAU DU DÉVELOPPEMENT DURABLE VILLE DE MONTRÉAL

p. 99: Sustainable Montréal 2016–2020, p. 8 diagram.

GETTY IMAGES

pp. viii, 2–3: © Donald Iain Smith; pp. viii, 28–29: © Kidstock; pp. viii, 102–103: © pchyburrs; pp. ix, 156–157: © Donald Iain Smith.

IDEO.ORG

p. 22: IDEO diagram.

SHUTTERSTOCK

pp. ix, 128–129: © 1000 Words; p. 3: © Macrovector; p. 4: © Khaled ElAdawy; p. 6 middle: © photofriday; p. 6 bottom left: mattxfoto; p. 6 bottom right: Ivana Perosevic; p. 7: © Leonel Calara; p. 8: © Rawpixel.com; p. 11: © Dmitry_Skvortsov; p. 12: © Inspired By Maps; p. 14: © Meunierd; p. 16: © Ritu Manoj Jethani; p. 17: © Robert Kneschke; p. 18: © Dean Drobot; p. 19: © Picsfive; p. 20: © Rawpixel.com; p. 23: © g-stockstudio; p. 25: © TuiPhotoEngineer; p. 26: © Rawpixel.com; p. 27: © Arttabula; p. 29: © Vector Goddess; p. 30: © rnkadsgn; p. 32 top: © MAGNIFIER; p. 32 bottom: © Danaan; p. 34: © Andreas Virviescas; p. 36: © dherrmann79; p. 37: © Singkham; p. 38: © lassedesignen; p. 39: © antoniomas; p. 41: © MikeDotta; p. 43: © WAYHOME studio; p. 45: © lev radin; p. 49: © Thanun Patiparnthada; p. 50: © Rawpixel.com; p. 51: ©Hyejin Kang; p. 52: © iMoved Studio; p. 53: © EXPLORER; p. 55: © Telnov Oleksii; p. 56: © alphaspirit; p. 57: © Anatoli Styf; p. 58: © Sergey Nivens; p. 60: © Andrey Arkusha; p. 63: © TreasureGalore; p. 64: © Rawpixel.com; p. 67: © drumdredd777; p. 68: © pichetw; p. 69: © Rawpixel.com; p. 70: © TZIDO SUN; p. 71: © Jacob Lund; p. 73: © MriMan; p. 75: © Igor Sinkov; p. 76: © Augustino; p. 77: © Rawpixel.com; p. 79 © elenabsi; p. 80: © Pressmaster; p. 81: © Andrey_Popov; p. 82: © santypan; p. 86: © S_Photo; p. 87: © Fettullah OZASLAN; p. 88: © mervas; p. 89: © MAGNIFIER; p. 90: © ReneeFoskett; p. 93: © Matipon; p. 94: © Rawpixel.com; p. 96: © Jakgapong Pengjank; p. 100: © petovarga; p. 101: © lassedesignen; p. 103: © Soloma; p. 104: © apiguide; p. 106: © Ollyy; p. 107: © Tiko Aramyan; p. 108: © taviphoto; p. 111: © Alta Oosthuizen; p. 112: © Danko Mykola; p. 114: © Tetyana Dotsenko; p. 117: © Fedorov Oleksiy; p. 118 middle: © Larissa Kulik; p. 118 bottom: © Dragon Images; p. 120: © fotoslaz; p. 122: © Bangokhappiness; p. 125: © Africa Studio; p. 126 middle: © yut548; p. 126 bottom left: © Ollyy; p. 129: © Bloomicon; p. 130: © metamorworks; p. 131: © DW labs Incorporated; p. 133: © qvist; p. 134: © Everett Historical; p. 135: © stockphoto mania; p. 137: © Pavle Bugarski; p. 138: © pathdoc; p. 140: © 1000 words; p. 144: © Ian Warren; p. 147: © Michael Moloney; p. 148: © maicasaa; p. 149: © GaudiLab; p. 150: © 4 PM production; p. 153: © dennizn; p. 154: © Prostock-studio; p. 157: © Bloomicon; p. 158: © wavebreakmedia; p. 160: © oatawa; p. 162: © Zapp2photo; p. 165: © GrandeDuc; p. 166: ©Monkey Business Images; p. 167: © Neil Lockhart; p. 168: © Lightspring; p. 171: © charles taylor; p. 172: © John Arehart; p. 173: © SFIO CRACHO; p. 174: © adike; p. 177: © Jeff Cameron Collingwood; p. 178: ©Jacob Lund; p. 180: © Rawpixel.com; p. 181: © pathdoc; p. 183: © Elegant Solution; p. 185: © Prostock-studio; p. 186: © pathdoc; p. 187: © elleon; p. 188: © tzuky333; p. 189 middle: © Attila JANDI; p. 189 bottom left: © Marco Uliana; p. 189 bottom centre: © Eric Isselee; p. 189 bottom right: © a9photo; p. 191: © Mylmages – Micha; p. 192: © Francesco Scatena; p. 194: © Art Babych; p. 199: © Dmytro Zinkevych; p. 200: © hafakot; p. 201: © sv_tdbr; p. 205: © ginger_polina_bublik; p. 206: © Michael Zysman; p. 207: © Haywiremedia; p. 208: © Rawpixel.com; p. 209: © Dieter Hawlan.

UNSPLASH

pp. viii, 54–55: © Matthew Henry; pp. viii, 78–79: © Jilbert Ebrahimi; pp. ix, 182–183: © Caroline Hernandez.

TEXT CREDITS

CHAPTER 6

p. 145 "Editorial Gatekeeping in Citizen Journalism" by A. M. Lindner. © 2016, New Media and Society. p. 146 "Sweat So You Don't Forget: Exercise Breaks during a University Lecture Increase On-Task Attention and Learning" by B. Fenesi, K. Lucibello, J. J. Heisz, & J. A. Kim. *Journal of Applied Research in Memory and Cognition*.

CHAPTER 8

p. 209 "Sex, Disease, and Extinction: What Ancient DNA Tells Us about Humans and Neanderthals" by R. Becker. *The Verge*, October 9, 2017. https://www.theverge.com/2017/10/9/16448412/neanderthal-stone-age-human-genes-dna-schizophrenia-cholesterol-hair-skin-loneliness.

AUDIO AND VIDEO CREDITS

CHAPTER 1

p. 7 "The State of Innovation" © Canadian Broadcasting Corporation. p. 12 "Manipulation Has Been Driving Innovation for Ages" © Canadian Broadcasting Corporation. p. 20 "Design Thinking" © Stanford University, Hoover Institute.

CHAPTER 2

p. 32 "Reimagining Business in Latin America" © Agora Partnerships. p. 38 "Capitalism on Steroids" © Canadian Broadcasting Corporation. p. 45 "Poverty Is a Threat to Peace" Yunus, Muhammad. Nobel Lecture [video podcast]. Oslo, December 10, 2006. © The Nobel Foundation.

CHAPTER 3

p. 58 "Is Your Genetic Privacy Safe?" © Canadian Broadcasting Corporation. p. 64 "Privacy, Consent, and Investigative Journalism" © Canadian Broadcasting Corporation. p. 71 "Protecting Our Neuroprivacy" © Canadian Broadcasting Corporation.

CHAPTER 4

p. 82 "Are Connected Bikes Key to Improving Urban Planning?" © Canadian Broadcasting Corporation. p. 89 "Sustainability: The Next Management Frontier (Part 1)" © MIT TechTV. p. 95 "Sustainability: The Next Management Frontier (Part 2)" © MIT TechTV.

CHAPTER 5

p. 107 "Your Phone Is an Extension of Your Mind" © Canadian Broadcasting Corporation. p. 113 "Aphantasia: When the Mental Image Is Missing" © Canadian Broadcasting Corporation. p. 121 "Can a Computer Be Creative?" with permission from University of Kent, https://www.cs.kent.ac.uk/people/staff/akj22/.

CHAPTER 6

p. 133 "The Future of Journalism: Old Media Is Dying" © Inspirefest.com. p. 139 "How to Be a Citizen Journalist" © Canadian Broadcasting Corporation. p. 149 "The Evolution of Journalism and Tapping into Tech for Storytelling" © Oxford University Podcasts.

CHAPTER 7

p. 162 "Artificial Intelligence Insight from Deep Learning Godfather" © Canadian Broadcasting Corporation. p. 167 "Toward an Artificial Brain" © World Economic Forum. p. 174 "Merging Human Brains with AI" © Canadian Broadcasting Corporation.

CHAPTER 8

p. 188 "Jane Goodall on Environmental Ethics" © Canadian Broadcasting Corporation. p. 194 "The Legacy: An Elder's Vision for Our Sustainable Future" Suzuki, David. Talk given at the Perth International Arts Festival, Perth, Australia. November 16, 2010. 6:55–23:16 http://www.abc.net.au/tv/bigideas/stories/2010/11/16/3066634.htm used with permission from the David Suzuki Institute. p. 201 "Fifty Years of Watching Climate Change" © Canadian Broadcasting Corporation.